Understanding Children

BEHAVIOR, MOTIVES, AND THOUGHT

Jerome Kagan

Harvard University

   HARCOURT BRACE JOVANOVICH, INC.

New York   Chicago   San Francisco   Atlanta

ISBN: 0-15-592873-2

Library of Congress Catalog Card Number: 75-155789

Printed in the United States of America

ACKNOWLEDGMENTS FOR ILLUSTRATIONS

Front cover: Top left, Victoria Beller; top right, Ford Foundation, Elizabeth Wilcox; bottom, Carter Hamilton, DPI.
Back cover: Top, Ken Heyman; bottom, Susan McCartney.
Page
   2: Top, Ken Heyman; bottom, Marion Bernstein.
  80: Top, Carter Hamilton, DPI; bottom, Ken Heyman.
104: Adapted from E. J. Gibson, "Development of Perception: Discrimination of Depth Compared with Discrimination of Graphic Symbols," in J. C. Wright and J. Kagan, eds., *Basic Cognitive Processes in Children* (Monograph, Society for Research in Child Development, 1963).
127: From J. Kagan, L. Pearson, and L. Welch, "Conceptual Impulsivity and Inductive Reasoning," *Child Development* 37 (1966), 583–94.

EPIGRAPH

From Chapter One of *The Labyrinth of Solitude: Life and Thought in Mexico* by Octavio Paz. Translated from the Spanish by Lysander Kemp. Copyright © 1961 by Grove Press, Inc. Published by and reprinted by permission of Grove Press, Inc. and Penguin Books Ltd.

Preface

These two essays contain the reflections of a psychologist who is concerned with the frontier where psychology, education, and the art of child-rearing meet. They are an attempt to translate current psychological knowledge about children into practical suggestions for those adults most involved in the child's welfare. Although the book is intended primarily as a supplement for courses in developmental and educational psychology, it is hoped that its message will reach the larger community of in-service teachers, parents, and other adults who are interested in and puzzled by the young.

The book stresses motivation and thought, because the changing profile of the child's desires and assumptions tells us the most about him. Unfortunately, these two processes are among the most puzzling to psychologists and consequently generate honest and often heated controversy. Moreover, scientific attempts to learn more about psychological growth have been hampered by the nineteenth-century prejudice that man is a simple sum of his actions, feelings, and thoughts—a view that allowed several generations of psychologists to rationalize their efforts to understand only one of these components of man. This book argues that each person's beliefs form the axis around which his motives, emotions, and behaviors are organized and function as the binding force in his personality.

The central theme of the first essay is that the need *to know* is insatiable and is continually forcing the child to rearrange his ideas into the most reasonable pattern. He wants information about tomorrow's challenges, the logic of his conclusions, and the fit between his behavioral strivings and his conception of the goals those

iii

actions serve. Since both his beliefs and his environment are in permanent flux, the child is always a little off balance. The strategies he employs to right himself form the story line of his development. Since age, cultural setting, and historical period dictate what beliefs are reasonable, the public aspects of the child's personality vary with each of these background dimensions.

The second essay, which is an analytic discussion of thought, defines the basic units and processes involved in cognition and argues that appreciation of these psychological qualities can aid the adult who works with children. It is hoped that the lengthy section on the nature of concepts will provide the teacher, in particular, with a framework for presentation of new ideas, regardless of the subject matter content.

Although the themes of *Understanding Children* have implications for psychiatry, clinical psychology, and education, most of the practical suggestions are addressed specifically to the teacher. I have tried throughout to offer clear and concrete suggestions for classroom application that logically flow from the theoretical discussion. I view education as an intricate and delicate ballet between partners who need and respect each other. Workbooks, machines, and visual aids merely provide the setting for the central drama. The aims of education have been distorted by the cultism that has grown out of the confusion of purpose that has characterized the last two decades. We have mistaken the novel for the valid, and slogans for axioms. To educate a child one must arrange conditions that permit him to commit himself to the creative use of mind; and people, not objects, are the most persuasive agents whenever one is proselytizing a faith. The strongest plea in these essays is to put the teacher back into education and to slow the accelerated trend toward isolating the child from the richest source of guidance, ideas, and values available to him.

I wish to express my appreciation to Professor Jacob W. Getzels for his helpful critique of the manuscript. I would like also to thank Mrs. Doris Simpson and Mrs. Judith Ross for their assistance in its preparation and the Carnegie Corporation of New York for enabling me to be free of academic duties for a year so that I could complete the first draft.

Jerome Kagan

Contents

Thought, 80

All of us, at some moment, have had a vision of our existence as something unique, untransferable and very precious. This revelation almost always takes place during adolescence. Self-discovery is above all the realization that we are alone: it is the opening of an impalpable, transparent wall—that of our consciousness—between the world and ourselves. It is true that we sense our aloneness almost as soon as we are born, but children and adults can transcend their solitude and forget themselves in games or work. The adolescent, however, vacillates between infancy and youth, halting for a moment before the infinite richness of the world. He is astonished at the fact of his being, and this astonishment leads to reflection: as he leans over the river of his consciousness, he asks himself if the face that appears there, disfigured by the water, is his own. The singularity of his being, which is pure sensation in children, becomes a problem and a question.

Octavio Paz

The Labyrinth of Solitude

Behavior and Motives

Each society must solve three basic problems —developing ways to care for the infant and child, establishing rules that govern how people should interact with one another, and transmitting skills and values from the adult to the youth. Our own society has had difficulty meeting the last requirement because, unlike less technological cultures, it established schools. In doing so, it relegated part of the responsibility for the training of the child to strangers and forced the child to learn skills that, strictly speaking, were not essential to meeting the demands of each day.

The Bushman child in the Kalahari Desert learns how to hunt, track, and ride a horse, abilities so obviously important to his survival that he does not need any special incentive to master them. Unfortunately, the subjects taught in public schools do not possess this quality of obvious necessity because, until recently, the major function of the school was to prepare a priest class. During the last three hundred years attendance at school has been primarily a ritual designed to preserve distinctions among social classes and to lend a mystique to those who successfully withstood its rigors. Although the American view of public school has always been more practical and democratic than that of the European, until the early part of this century Americans never seriously believed that school success was a prerequisite to economic security. The role of the American public school was one of helping the family build character in young children. The school extended and supplemented the moral values of the parents and insisted on obedience to authority, control of strong passions, and faith in God. Both school and family regarded the critical function of public education to be the molding of responsible citizens. Only eighty years ago Horace Mann wrote:

> Educate, only educate enough and we shall regenerate the criminal and eradicate vice; through the schools we shall teach mankind to moderate their passions and develop their virtues. (Quoted in Hardy, p. 5.)

This emphasis on character training was so strong that a passionate involvement in mathematics was regarded as an unhealthy trait. The heroes of the young were George Washington, Thomas Jefferson, and Benjamin Franklin, honest men who served their fellow citizens with sincerity and loyalty. The mission of education was to supply society with a cadre of similar heroes by preparing the young to assume roles of benevolent leadership.

In every community a small group of men must assume responsibility for the general welfare of others, be it the guardianship of their health or legal prerogatives, their spiritual enlightenment, or their protection from enemies. Each individual must be ready to surrender part of his sovereignty to those who assume these roles of wisdom. The benevolent leaders of the society should possess three qualities. They must be able to put aside the natural desire for immediate gratification in order to work toward a "better" goal in the future. They must be honest and capable of assuming responsibility. Finally, they must be willing to commit themselves to abstract principles.

A society can fill these essential roles in a limited number of ways. When the group is small the positions can be inherited; but in larger groups other procedures of selection must be developed. Western society invented, and has used with profit, a work-sample test to choose its leaders. Our society assumes that any person who persists in the educational system for sixteen to twenty years with acceptable levels of performance and no sins on his record is more likely to possess the desired attributes of a leader than one who never began the arduous journey or who withdrew before it was over. Since the system worked efficiently, our society was not concerned with early school failures. Early failures simply indicated how sensitive the procedure was in eliminating those who did not have the proper temperament or ability to take responsibility for their fellow man.

We live today in a different era, the first period in history in which a minimum of twelve years of formal education is necessary for personal dignity and economic survival. Hence most citizens have become concerned with the many early failures that were ignored in the past. We now realize that these failures form the basis for serious psychological illness in the entire society, and we are ready to make changes in the educational system. Indeed, the many books and articles written on the subject suggest that change in any form should be beneficial. But we still hold to the time-tested notion that selection of the proper remedy is most likely to follow from accurate diagnosis of the problem. We must first understand the deficiencies in our educational system before we can initiate major changes in its procedures. This book is an attempt to illuminate the problem by examining the child and his relationships with those adults who are eager to mold him into their image of maturity.

As parents or teachers, we want children to display certain behaviors in school, particularly persistence with difficult problems and reasonable obedience to adult requests. We also insist that children learn the language and number skills that are prerequisites for the study of technical vocations, as well as for the filling out of tax forms. In addition, we want every child to expect ultimate success in a problem if he invests reasonable effort. The child must come to believe that he will learn a new talent if he tries. Finally, we want children to be motivated to perfect their abilities and to develop new ones.

Many children do not readily adopt these behaviors, beliefs, skills, and motives, and we wonder why. We know that the six-year-old is a malleable creature, continually modifying his actions and opinions, and we are puzzled by his resistance to adopting the characteristics we care so much about. A person will learn a new skill and practice it if he believes, first, that he has a chance of mastering it and, second, that the mastery will bring him a desired goal. Many children enter school with neither the confidence that they will succeed nor the belief that learning to read or write will lead to some prize. Hence it is difficult to tempt the child to work at developing these talents.

There are two strategies that can be used to persuade the child to invest more effort in school. The first technique works directly on his motivation. We can tell the child that he cannot have certain goals unless he learns the skills we value. Praise, acceptance, and the perception of similarity to an attractive adult model are three significant sources of motivation for the child, and many schools consciously manipulate the child's relation to the teacher so that these motives are more fully exploited. We shall return to this strategy later.

The second technique that can be used to persuade the child to learn involves coercion. Most schools adopt a Puritan attitude, acting as though they believed the school were inherently unattractive. They coerce the child into learning certain skills, trusting that if he is successful he will eventually come to enjoy them. This argument has some merit. If a child is forced to play the piano and eventually becomes expert at it, he is likely to develop an affection for this activity. He will want to practice! Similarly, the giving of an examination, the support of an army, and the playing of cards in a summer cabin can begin as reactions to specific external pressures. If adults practice these actions long enough, they may develop a preference for them. Many schools implicitly adopt this philosophy. Teach the child reading, spelling, and adding, and if he eventually masters these tasks he will learn to like them.

This plan does not work all the time because people are more likely to practice an action when they *select* the task to be mastered than when they are *forced* to work at a task chosen by others. For example, if every urban citizen were required by law to travel every summer weekend to a crowded seaside resort over a highway of bumper-to-bumper traffic for four hours, it is unlikely that he would want to make the trip as often as he does when he has the option to choose that form of holiday. There is no need to invent a reason for traveling to the seashore if one is forced to do so by law. But if a person has the choice, then he must create a reason for enduring the frustrations of the trip, and the delights of surf and sand are sufficient. People are more likely to assume that their actions derive from personal motives when they believe they have freely selected the goal-related actions. Under these conditions, each person must explain his behavior to himself, and he does so by assuming that he wanted what he worked so hard to attain. Neither children nor adults will invent a motive to explain their actions if they believe that they have been coerced.

The child is usually forced to learn the academic skills of reading, adding, and spelling and feels no need to make up a reason for working at these tasks. Since he is not given the opportunity to decide for himself that these are desirable talents, he may not develop a strong motive for mastering them. He has an easier explanation: "Teachers and parents make me go" is the typical reply to the question "Why do you go to school?" This perception of external pressure has two consequences. It obstructs the development of a motive to master academic tasks, and it breeds resistance to the entire school environment. It might be wise therefore to devote part of the first grade to creating conditions that would enable the child to decide for himself that learning to read, write, and spell were good things to do, rather than telling him so autocratically. Such a procedure, if successful, might wed the child's natural excitement to the missions of education.

Behavior and Identity

PROCESSES OF BEHAVIOR CHANGE

Since adults want to mold the child's behavior in accordance with their conception of maturity, it is useful to consider the factors that produce changes in behavior. There are two meanings to the phrase "behavior change." The first refers to an increase in the frequency of a behavior that the child already knows how to display but will not do so as often as we would like or in the places that we designate. The child knows how to speak but sits quietly in class; he knows how to attend to the teacher but chooses to ignore her; he knows how to wait his turn but demands that he go first. In each of these examples, the desired action does not have to be taught. Rather, the child has to be persuaded to exhibit the actions *more often* and under the proper circumstances.

The second meaning of "behavior change" refers to the learning of a truly new response or skill, one that the child does not yet possess. We want to teach the child to write his name, to sketch a human figure, to bisect an angle. Of course, every new behavior must be built from fragments of existing ones; but teaching a new response often involves the gradual organization of the new skill, whereas merely increasing the occurrence of an existing response involves changing the child's motivation and decreasing any inhibitions about performing the act. Three processes are involved in changing overt behavior: direct instruction, reinforcement, and observation of others.

Direct Instruction. Direct instruction is the simplest way to alter behavior. Anyone can change a child's behavior by telling him what to do, as long as the child understands the instruction and wants to comply. The sand-lot coach's command "Hold your right hand over your left hand, keep your feet apart, and swing when the ball is in front of your bat" states explicitly what the young batsman should do, and such instruction facilitates display of the new skill. Instruction alone can aid the learning of many new actions, but it is usually more effective when the child's responses are attended by discernible feedback, or reinforcement.

Reinforcement. It is a basic psychological principle that a person's tendency to display an action is dependent on certain events that follow the action. These "special" events are called *reinforcements.* Positive reinforcements, or rewards, are events the child desires, and they lead to increases in the frequency of an act; negative reinforcements are events the child regards as undesirable, and they lead to decreases in the frequency of an act. The use of praise, report cards, after-school punishment, or teaching machines is based, either explicitly or implicitly, on the principle that the child wants more positive reinforcements and fewer negative ones.

It is important to realize that the word "reinforcement" is defined only in terms of an effect on behavior, not on the basis of independent criteria. A reinforcement is any event—no matter how strange—that alters the frequency of an action. If a child's mother pops balloons every time he practices the piano and thereby makes the child practice longer, balloon-popping is a reinforcement. Thus any event in the world is a potential reinforcement. But the only way to determine if it is, is to try it and see whether or not it alters some action. The definition of a reinforcement is relative and dependent upon the behavior of the individual. This notion may be clarified by an analogy to the meaning of the word "dawn." We usually define dawn in absolute terms, as a change from darkness to light in the eastern part of the sky. If we were to define dawn as the time of day when people begin to arise from sleep, in the twenty-four-hour darkness of the Scandinavian winter dawn would exist in a pitch-black sky. Perhaps we can obtain a better understanding of the nature of a reinforcement by noting what happens when a reinforcement occurs.

First, a reinforcement typically interrupts an ongoing stream of behavior and directs the child's attention to a specific response he has just made. For example, a young child is painting and has just drawn a window on a house when suddenly the teacher says, "That's very good, John." This unexpected interruption of the behavior breaks the chain of action at the point where a particular response has just occurred—in this case, the drawing of a window. The direction of the child's attention is changed and becomes focused on the action he has just completed and on his thoughts about that action. The act of sketching the window is now more salient to him than if the teacher had not spoken. A reinforcement is like an arrow on a map; it points to a specific locus and invites the attentional system to focus its energy there.

Second, a reinforcement sets up a problem in prediction. Children continually try to predict the occurrence of events in their environment, especially those that are unusual or unexpected. A child tries to predict when his mother will be angry with him, when his father will come home, when lightning will strike. Psychological experiments have shown that if a child is given a piece of candy every time he selects the correct answer in a learning problem, he will often try to control the delivery of the candies until he has figured out the secret of the schedule. Once he understands the relation between his actions and the reinforcing candies, he may stop behaving. In difficult learning problems that require a hundred or more trials for mastery, the child may stop responding after thirty or forty trials, just when he seems to be solving the problem. Psychologists often explain this phenomenon by saying that the child is tired of the reinforcement, that he is not motivated for it. In many cases, however, the reason for the child's boredom is not satiation with the candies but satisfaction of his curiosity about what controls their occurrence. He can predict when they will be delivered, and so he stops playing the game. It is not the candy that he wants but *the certainty of knowing how to get it*. The formal games that produce the strongest loyalties—such as poker, chess, and bridge—are those in which the outcome is difficult to predict. Children complain about games or events that can be "figured out" too easily. The well-worn dictum about "not praising every action" owes its validity to the fact that inconsistent praise makes the prediction problem more challenging for the child.

Some psychologists use reinforcements to alleviate childhood symptoms like shyness. Rewarding an excessively shy girl by a pat on the shoulder every time she approaches another child can produce dramatically positive results. This type of strategy is called *behavior therapy*. But the effects might be diluted if the child knew exactly when each reinforcement would be delivered and were certain that she would be touched affectionately with minimal effort. The puzzle surrounding when the rewards occur would be solved and the motive for continuing the behavior might be weakened.

Some reinforcements are of course inherently pleasant, emotionally exciting events. A light touch, a sweet taste, a tickle, a rhythmic ride on an adult's lap all generate strong, pleasant sensations that the child wants to experience again and again. But most children learn to read and write without being given candy or kisses. Hence the facilitating effect of reinforcements rests heavily on processes other than sensory pleasure.

In sum, a reinforcement focuses the child's attention on the action he has just made, tempts him to figure out the schedule of its occurrence, and emotionally excites him. A reinforcement is a punctuation mark in the stream of experience that accents a particular thought or activity. It carves an action out of the flux of ongoing behavior, brings it to the front of consciousness, and binds it to the context and the psychological state existing at the moment.

Observation of Others. Since the recruitment of attention to an action is perhaps the most important effect of a reinforcement, it is not surprising that a child can be taught a new response, or can learn to change an existing one, merely by watching someone else perform the desired action. In an ingenious experiment, a group of cats was taught to press a lever each time a light went on in order to obtain milk. A second group of cats was allowed to watch the first group learn to press the lever to obtain the milk. When these "observer" cats were placed in the box with the lever, they learned the behavior more easily than the cats who were trained in the traditional way, with milk as a reinforcement. (John *et al.*, 1968.)

Children probably learn more ideas and skills by watching and listening to others than by any other mechanism. The best example of this principle is the acquisition of language.

Changing the child's behavior through observation is easiest when the child already knows how to exhibit the desired response and we simply wish to alter its frequency. If the behavior is complex and the child does not possess all the subunits, he must be given ample opportunity to practice each action. The child cannot learn to ski, swim, or write an essay through observation alone. He will have to display each subunit of the behavior in its early, crude form, eliminate those actions that are obstructive or irrelevant, and then polish the behavior. The use of reward in this process is helpful.

The child does not watch all people with equal care, selectivity, or motivation, and there are reasons for his preferences. What are the factors that determine whether a child will observe another person, whom he will observe, and more important, which of the model's actions, motives, and values he will adopt? First, the child often orients to those people from whom he has come to expect guidance, affection, and help. If he is unsure of himself, he is likely to orient to those adults who have been affectionate and useful in the past. Second, the child orients to those adults who have power over him, who might punish, dominate, or hurt him. Some children grow up in a family setting in which they are consistently disciplined, verbally or physically, for a list of misdemeanors ranging from touching a vase to teasing a younger sister. Years of reprimand make a child vigilant; they put him on guard against the unexpected blow from behind. Many children have an automatic habit of glancing toward an adult when they are near a place they think may be off limits or when they are about to initiate a forbidden action. They look briefly to the adult's face, searching for a sign that says either "stop" or "go ahead." These hypervigilant children can be helped by being given a clear understanding of what is forbidden and what is allowed, so that they do not have to live in an atmosphere of continual uncertainty. Such children also need to change their perception of the adult from that of a policeman with a club to that of a reasonable judge whose warnings and punishments are rational and can be anticipated.

Finally, the child usually orients to those people who possess physical or psychological attributes he admires. Most children believe that strength, power over others, physical attractiveness, warmth, honesty, sincerity, and a rich collection of abilities are good and valuable traits, and they are attracted to adults who command these characteristics. The child is drawn to adults who are kind to him, or potentially capable of kindness, and to those whom he respects or believes others respect. The child imitates these heroic adults. This universal phenomenon introduces the concept of identification.

IDENTIFICATION

A six-year-old boy feels good when he hears a visitor congratulate his father on a promotion or overhears a neighbor comment on his father's youthful vigor. A five-year-old girl feels shame when she learns that her mother has deserted the family, has attempted suicide, and is now in a mental hospital. In each of these examples, the child's emotions seem more appropriate to the parent than to the child. However, the child acts as though he were the parent. The proud six-year-old boy feels as if he, and not his father, had been congratulated; the five-year-old girl suffers as if she, and not her mother, had been hospitalized for the attempted suicide. This phenomenon of vicarious sharing in the emotional states of those to whom one feels similar is called *identification.*

Why should the child feel emotions that are in actuality appropriate to someone else? Identification stems from the child's belief that some of the attributes of another person, or model, belong to him. The model can be a parent, a sibling, a relative, a friend, or a fictional character. A boy who realizes that he and his father have the same name and the same bright red hair and is told by all his relatives that he and his father have warm, hearty laughs comes to believe that he is similar in a fundamental way to that parent. When this belief in physical and psychological similarity permits the child to experience emotions appropriate to the father, the child is said to have established an identification with him.

How Identification Is Established and Strengthened. Children do not develop strong identifications with everyone to whom they feel similar. Moreover, they can develop identifications with more than one model. Four related processes are involved in the establishment and strengthening of an identification.

Process 1: The perception of similarity to a model. Every child believes that he shares physical or psychological characteristics with some other person. The greater the number of characteristics believed to be shared and the more distinctive those characteristics, the firmer the child's belief that he is similar to the model. Thus perceived similarity in unusual attributes contributes in a major way to the establishment of an identification. If a characteristic is possessed by everyone, like two eyes or five fingers, the child does not attribute much importance to it. If the shared attribute is relatively uncommon, like freckles or bright red hair, the child is likely to invest it with much value.

There are three ways in which the child can amplify the belief that he is similar to a model. In the first and most primitive mechanism, he recognizes that he and the model have certain features in common. In the case of the father, the boy knows that they have the same last name and perhaps the same first name. He also notes that they have the same sexual anatomy, are upset by the same irritating events, or have the same facial birthmark. The child also awards enormous value to the blood relationship between his parents and himself, since this is unique to his family. A second way in which the child develops a belief in similarity to a model is through the active adoption, often by imitation, of the model's behavior, opinions, and dress. A young girl may adopt her mother's moral values, her taste in clothes, or her interactive style with the father and in so doing will strengthen her presumption of similarity to her mother. Finally, the child's belief in his similarity to a model is strengthened by those adults who tell him that he is similar to the model.

In most cases, all three mechanisms lead the child inevitably to the conclusion that he is more similar to his same-sex biological parent than to any other adult he knows. Hence boys usually develop the strongest identifications with their fathers and girls identify most strongly with their mothers.

Process 2: The experience of vicarious affect. Whenever a child experiences an emotion that is appropriate to the model, the child is said to be sharing vicariously in the affective state of the model. A girl who enjoys seeing her father kiss her mother or a boy who becomes excited by seeing his father's name in the newspaper is experiencing vicarious affect. *An identification exists between a child and a model whenever the child believes that he is similar to the model and shares in the model's emotions.* In effect, the child seems to believe that events that occur to the model also occur to him. This process leads the child to believe that people will react to him as he thinks they react to the model.

Process 3: The desire for the model's attractive attributes. The young child is sure that most adults, especially his parents, are physically stronger, more competent, and wiser than he is and have greater freedom of choice and opportunities for pleasure than are available to him. The child wants these attractive privileges for himself. He wants to be smarter and stronger than he is; he wants to be able to dominate others, to resist coercion, to decide where he will sleep and when he will eat. The child is also attracted to the model's physical ability and skills. He wants to be able to lift heavy objects, drive a car, swim in deep water, and operate a power mower. Finally, the child is attracted to a model whom he perceives as kind and affectionate toward others. Thus the attractiveness of the model is based on his potency, ability, and humanity.

Process 4: Imitation of the model. The child tries to adopt the beliefs, values, and behaviors of the model because he believes that by increasing their similarity he will be able to gain some of the model's less tangible psychological attributes, such as power, popularity, and skill. The child seems to assume that if two people are alike on external traits, they must also share similar psychological attributes. The greater the obvious external similarity between child and model, the stronger the child's expectation that he will be able to gain the less tangible psychological qualities he values—the model's power, affection, attractiveness, and competence. The desire for these qualities motivates the child to imitate the model's behaviors and assume his values and motives.

A young man recalls his childhood feelings for his father:

> My admiration for him transcended everything. I always wanted to work with my hands on machinery, to drive big trucks, to fix things like he did. I didn't really like spinach but I never lost the image of his bathtub filled with it, and up to a few years ago I always ate it—it was good for me and would make me strong, like him. (Goethals and Klos, p. 44.)

Interrelationship of the processes. The relationships among these four processes form the basis for two important principles. First, the child who believes that he is similar to another person is likely to experience vicarious emotions appropriate to that model.

These two conditions, as we have seen, define identification. Second, the child tries to adopt the model's attributes in order to increase the similarity between them and to gain more of the model's desirable characteristics. The more successfully he imitates the model, the stronger his belief in their similarity becomes and the more likely he is to experience vicarious emotions. Thus the desire for the model's attributes and imitation of the model strengthen identification. Every time the child imitates the model, by adopting an action or taking on an attitude, his belief in their essential similarity becomes firmer and it becomes easier for him to share vicariously in the model's successes.

In general, the more desirable the model's attributes, the greater the likelihood that the child will strive to become like the model. Since the adoption of the model's characteristics increases perceived similarity, the child will experience even more intense vicarious emotions. If this cycle of increased similarity and vicarious emotion continues for many years, the child may become so closely bound to the model that he will believe that a part of himself is permanently invested in the admired person.

Identification and Deviant Development. The fact that the child develops beliefs, motives, and behaviors that reflect dominant cultural values is easier to explain than the fact that he adopts beliefs or actions that *deviate from the norm.* We can explain normative behaviors without resorting to the concept of identification. The child sits in school, runs in the playground, and talks at the lunch table, behaviors that are appropriate in these contexts and not necessarily based on identification. Similarly, the act of making the bed each morning is usually based on a desire to avoid parental criticism rather than on an identification with a parent. Most of the behaviors the child displays each day are either habitual reactions to a particular setting or actions motivated by a wish to attain a reward, avoid punishment, or master a culturally valued skill. However, these mechanisms will not explain why a five-year-old whose parents praise obedience and punish disobedience is rebellious; why a ten-year-old who has been told that his father deserted the family shows a sudden loss of motivation in school; or why a thirty-five-year-old woman whose mother became schizophrenic at age thirty-six becomes anxious and insomniac, as if she believed that she too were about to go insane. These actions are appropriate to no particular context; nor do they bring joy and postpone pain. Rather, they flow from beliefs about one's fundamental attributes that were established through identification with a model.

Development of the Self-Concept. Identification not only has a profound influence on behavior; it also plays an important role in the development of the ambiguous process of self-definition, often called the *self-concept.* The child's self-concept consists in part of his evaluation of the degree to which his attributes match those that the culture regards as good. The valued attributes in our culture include, among others, warmth, sincerity, honesty, strength, size, physical attractiveness, intelligence, autonomy, sexual potency, wealth, power, and a capacity to enjoy life. The child's sense of the degree to which he possesses these "good" attributes is determined in part by his social experiences. For instance, his evaluation of his power or strength is based to some extent on his ability to defeat a rival in a game or fight, to resist pressure, and to dominate others. But the child is also prone to regard himself positively or negatively on the basis of his identification with various models. A boy who has identified with a handsome father regards himself as more attractive; a girl who has identified with a courageous mother feels bolder.

A negative view of the self is established if the child identifies with a model who possesses undesirable attributes. Most five-year-olds, confronted with the fact that they are more similar to their same-sex parent than to any other adult (because they share the same surname, body build, genitals, and certain unique features), will develop a minimal identification with that parent. This identification occurs regardless of how undesirable or unattractive the parent may be, for it is impossible to believe one shares nothing with biological parents. To be of the same "flesh and blood" as another is to possess an unalterable bond of shared identity. As the child begins to recognize the negative qualities of the parental model, he comes to believe that some of these qualities must be inherent in his personality.

A basic determinant of serious mental disorder is the belief that one shares similarities with a parent who has bad traits. This belief leads the child or adult to conclude that he too is hateful, mean, aggressive, disturbed, weak, irresponsible, unintelligent, unpopular, or incapable of expressing warmth and affection. Many unhappy adults feel unworthy, incompetent or undesirable because they believe they are fundamentally similar to a parent with these traits. A schizophrenic woman does not want to feel she is as cold, hateful, or selfish as her mother, but the identification that occurred twenty years earlier cannot be denied.

The average child identifies first with his parents, for they are the adults whom he knows best and whom he first respects and admires. As he grows older, he evaluates his parents' power and competence in perspective, for he meets and hears about other adults with qualities that surpass those of his parents. He reads about great athletes, astronauts, and scientists. The powerful motivation required to work on a scientific discovery or a novel is often based on an identification with a relevant model, and the commitment to the work is an attempt to maximize similarity to that model. The child is more likely to believe he can command power and glory if someone of his own sex, ethnic, religious, or racial group has done so in the past. These bases for perceived similarity often catalyze attempts to "be like" the model.

In the current civil-rights struggle, black leaders recognize that the young black child has difficulty perceiving similarity to white adults and therefore of establishing an identification with white heroes and white culture. The black child must be exposed to attractive black models if he is to develop a firm concept of himself and an expectation that he too can assume roles of extraordinary power, creativity, and humanity. The movement to celebrate the beauty of blackness and to place talented black adults in positions of power and responsibility should have a beneficial effect on the black child's attitudes toward his own competence and worthiness. It is also reasonable to assume that many black children will benefit from being taught by black teachers. Other things equal, the black child is more likely to identify with a black model than a white model and to strive to adopt the model's values. Thus, if intellectual competence is one of the teacher's values, the average black child will be more quickly persuaded of the validity of that ideal by a black teacher.

This last recommendation is but one instance of a more general principle. All teachers are potential models, and their power to sculpt values is underestimated. The early school years have an important propaganda function. The teacher must persuade the child of the joy, beauty, and potential utility of knowledge that does not seem to be of immediate relevance. The typical second grader does not agree with this idea. The teacher's most potent weapon of persuasion is herself. If she is seen as human, competent, and just—the major attributes of a heroine—the child will award to the tasks

17

she assigns the same reverence he assigns to her. As one first grader with such a teacher remarked, "Mrs. Stokes is such a nice person. She even got me to like numbers." The hiring of teachers is too often based on credentials having little to do with the potential to act as an effective model. It is easier to assess professional competence than humanity. But both administrators and teachers should bear in mind that the teacher, especially in the primary grades, is first a model and then a dispenser of knowledge.

SEX-ROLE IDENTITY AND STANDARDS

The personal definition of the self is a tangle of many dimensions, varying from weight and intelligence to wealth and political affiliation. Of the many attributes that are orchestrated into the self-concept, morality, competence, and sex-role integrity are of special importance. Each person wants to know how good, how talented, and how masculine or feminine he or she is. The answer to the last question defines the person's sex-role identity.

Stated formally, a *sex-role identity* is a belief concerning the degree to which a person's set of biological and psychological characteristics is congruent with his or her idealized view of the concept "male" or "female." The definition of the ideal—called a *sex-role standard*—is always influenced by the particular values of the culture. A Kyoto girl is taught that gentleness is the central feminine quality; a Los Angeles girl is taught that physical beauty is critical. In order to understand the significance of a sex-role identity in the shaping of behavior and motives four issues must be examined: (1) the content of the sex-role standards used to evaluate the self; (2) the implications of a firm versus a fragile sex-role identity; (3) the extent to which some standards generalize across cultures because of biological differences between the sexes; and (4) the significance of current changes in sex-role standards.

The Content of Sex-Role Standards. The child's learning of sex-role standards is not unlike his learning of other concepts. He learns that an object that is round, made of rubber, and bounces is called a "ball." He learns more about the definition of a ball by watching how it is used, listening to people talk about it, and playing with one. By age two, he has learned that certain objects are called "boys" and "men"; others "girls" and "women." He learns a more complete definition of male and female by noting what the sexes do, how they look, and what they say and by listening to others discuss the normative personalities of males and females. The categorization of human beings into male and female, usually present by two and a half years of age, is one of the earliest conceptual classifications made by the child.

The characteristics that define the sex roles include physical attributes, beliefs, feelings, motives, and public behaviors. Most American girls today regard an attractive face, hairless body, small frame, and moderate-sized breasts as ideal physical characteristics; boys regard height, large muscle mass, and facial and body hair as ideal.

The feminine sex-role standards for motives and emotions emphasize the ability to experience deep feelings, to gratify a love object, and to elicit sexual arousal in a male. A young woman's reminiscence of her first sexual experience captures the essence of these standards:

> Bob fell asleep on my chest with this great smile on his face, and I lay overwhelmed with tenderness and love for him. Then, thinking of the way he had looked at me, I was filled with awe that I could make him that happy, that I could move him that deeply. (Goethals and Klos, p. 280.)

The masculine standards for emotions and motives also emphasize the ability to gratify a love object, but they stress equally a pragmatic attitude, independence of judgment, and the ability to control expression of fear.

Aggression has been a primary sex-typed behavior in our culture. The traditional sex-role standard for behavior holds that girls and women should inhibit physical aggression but that boys and men should be free to express aggression when seriously threatened. It is difficult to find a psychological study in which aggressive behavior was not displayed more frequently among males than females. Children as well as adults regard males as more aggressive, dangerous, and punitive than females. This view also persists at a symbolic level, for six-year-olds believe that a tiger is a masculine animal, a rabbit feminine. If children are shown pictures depicting abstract qualities and asked to state which pictures are more like their father, their mother, or themselves, both boys and girls classify the father as darker, larger, more dangerous, and more angular than the mother. And boys classify themselves as darker, larger, more dangerous, and more angular than do girls. These views are not limited to English-speaking cultures, for Japanese, Navajo, and Mexican adults classify males as large, angular, and dark and women as small, round, and light. (Osgood, 1960.)

Dependency, passivity, and conformity are also sex-typed behaviors in our culture. Girls and women are generally allowed to express dependent behaviors, whereas boys and men are pressured to inhibit them. Thus men experience greater conflict over being passive and women experience greater conflict over being aggressive.

Differential conflict over aggressive and dependent behavior is reflected not only in action but also in reluctance to perceive this behavior in others. Middle-class American adults were shown a series of scenes in which an adult was acting either aggressively or dependently toward another. The pictures were shown at very fast speeds, ranging in duration from one-hundredth of a second to one second, and each person was asked to describe what he thought the pictures were about. The women had greater difficulty than the men recognizing the scenes that depicted aggression; the men had greater difficulty than the women recognizing the scenes that depicted dependency. Moreover, when each person was asked half an hour later to remember the pictures that he had seen, the women more readily recalled the dependency scenes and the men more readily recalled the aggressive scenes. (Kagan and Moss, 1962.)

Although intellectual ability is not as clearly a sex-typed characteristic as aggressive or dependent behavior, exceptional intellectual talent, particularly in science and mathematics, is more common among adolescent males than females. One reason for this sex-typing of ability is that academic excellence is necessary for vocational success and is therefore a more essential component of a man's identity. In addition, adolescent girls are more anxious over excessive intellectual competitiveness than boys. Many adolescents view intellectual striving as a form of aggressive behavior. Since sex-role standards discourage aggressive behavior in females, many young women inhibit intense intellectual effort. A visit to a college dining hall typically reveals male students arguing so intensely over a philosophical or scientific issue that the air seems to crackle with hostility. Equally intense debate among female students is less frequent because it is more threatening to their sex-role identity.

In the primary grades, however, girls typically outperform boys in all subject areas, and the ratio of boys to girls with reading problems ranges from 3 : 1 to 6 : 1. One reason for the relative superiority of girls in the primary grades is that the average American six-year-old perceives school as a feminine place. His introduction into school is usually monitored by female teachers who initiate the activities of painting, coloring, and singing and who place a premium on obedience and suppression of aggression and restlessness. The child perceives these values as more appropriate to girls than to boys. Groups of second-grade children were taught to associate different nonsense syllables with the concepts of male and female. They were then shown pictures of objects seen in school, such as a blackboard, a page of arithmetic, and a book, as well as pictures of objects unrelated to school life, and were asked to label the pictures with the "male" or "female" nonsense syllables. The children were more likely to label school objects feminine than masculine. (Kagan, 1964.)

Since many young boys perceive the school atmosphere as feminine, they resist complete involvement in classroom activities and fall behind girls in academic progress. If this hypothesis has merit, then a school with many male teachers should have a smaller proportion of boys than girls with serious reading problems. American communities like Akron, Ohio, are experimenting with such a plan. Boys begin to view knowledge as more appropriate to their sex as they approach adolescence and recognize that the masculine fields of engineering, science, accounting, and medicine require intellectual skills taught by the school.

Firmness of Sex-Role Identity.   Real objects in the world are most often defined by their physical appearance, their functions, and the conceptual categories to which they belong. A lemon is a small, round citrus fruit used for flavoring. The objective definitions of the human male and female emphasize a small set of biological, anatomical, and psychological characteristics, ranging from genetic constitution to hobbies. But man, unlike the lemon, defines himself to himself, and this subjective view is not identical with the definition in the dictionary.

It may seem odd that anyone should be unsure of his sex-role identity. A five-foot, eleven-inch eighteen-year-old named Robert with X and Y chromosomes, testes, penis, and body hair, is, by definition, a male. All such men should regard themselves as equally masculine. But the mind, in its perversity, does not completely trust these concrete physical signs and insists on including psychological evidence in its final judgment.

An individual's sex-role identity is a personal belief about his or her own maleness or femaleness and is not a simple derivative of how masculine or feminine his or her public behavior may be. As the child matures he comes to recognize the sex-role attributes that define masculinity and feminity in his cultural group. The child senses the degree to which his personality matches these standards. If the match is close and he desires it to be close, his sex-role identity will be firm. If the match is distant and he does not possess the sex-role characteristics he wants, his sex-role identity will be fragile.

Differences among children in the firmness of their sex-role identity arise from three sources. First, most children believe that they are more like their same-sex parent than any other adult and preferentially imitate that parent. A boy whose father is bold and athletic is more likely to believe he possesses those masculine attributes than a boy whose father has the opposite trait profile. Second, children are vulnerable to the special definition of sex-role identity shared by their peer group. A boy who is clumsy on the playing field is more likely to question his sex-role identity if his friends regard athletics as a salient masculine activity than if his friends value intellectual prowess.

Finally, the integrity of the sex-role identity is seriously dependent on the quality of sexual relationships in adolescence. The sex-role identity has two important periods of growth: the first occurs during the years prior to puberty, when acquisition of peer-valued sex-role characteristics is primary; the second occurs during adolescence, when success in heterosexual encounters is central. If the adolescent is unable to establish successful heterosexual relationships, he will begin to question his sex-role identity. The potential for attracting the affection of another person and entering into a satisfactory sexual union is the essence of the sex-role standard for the adult.

Each person continually tries to match his attributes to his notion of the ideal sex role. This urge to know about one's masculinity or feminity is only one facet of the more pervasive desire to gain as much information about the self as possible. If a person believes he is close to his standard, his spirits are buoyed; he is confident that he can come even closer, and he makes the attempt. If he feels he is far from his standard, he may turn away from it and accept the role of a "feminine" man (or a "masculine" woman). The decision to become homosexual, though laden with apprehension, can free a person from the awesome responsibilities of heterosexuality. Acceptance of a culturally inappropriate sex role reduces the terrible anxiety that comes from the recognition of serious deviation from an ideal that cannot be attained. The only possible solution is to redefine the ideal in terms of what can be attained.

Biological Factors and Sex-Role Development. Some of the sex differences seen in adults can be observed very early in development. Young girls are more likely than boys to stay close to their mothers when they are either apprehensive or bored. This writer has observed two-year-old boys and girls with their mothers in a large room decorated as a living room. Initially, the children were left in the room to become accustomed to the new situation. The girls stayed in closer physical contact with their mothers than the boys. Several toys were then brought into the room and the children were allowed to play for half an hour. Most of the children left their mothers immediately and began to play. However, after twenty minutes many children became bored and restless. The girls drifted back toward their mothers and the boys wandered around the room. One of the toys in this play situation was a clear plastic box about thirty inches on each side that very few of the children had seen before. Both the boys and the girls played with the box and put blocks or small objects in it. But the boys, and rarely the girls, tried to get into the box and close the cover over themselves—that is, the boys were more likely to use their body as an object of play.

It may be more than coincidence that the rhesus monkey and baboon, who are not taught sex-role standards, show sex differences resembling those observed in this study with children. Infant female monkeys stay closer to their mothers than do male monkeys. Moreover, display of threatening gestures and body-contact play is more frequent among young male than female monkeys, whereas passive withdrawal to stress is more common among females. These similarities force us to consider the possibility that some of the psychological differences between men and women may not be the product of experience alone but derivative of subtle biological differences between the sexes.

Sex differences with respect to certain intellectual abilities support this idea. At all ages, males usually perform slightly better than females on tests of spatial ability, whereas females do slightly better than males on tests of verbal ability. These differences have never been satisfactorily explained. The paired hemispheres of the brain have slightly different functions, with ability at nonverbal, spatial tasks more dependent on structures in the right hemisphere and language ability more dependent on structures in the left hemisphere. Normally the left hemisphere dominates the right. If the relative dominance of left over right hemisphere were established earlier in life in the female, this might account for the relative superiority of girls over boys in verbal skills during the primary grades. Dr. Herbert Lansdell of the National Institutes of Health has reported that removal of parts of the right temporal cortex in epileptic patients was more detrimental to spatial skills among males than females, suggesting that the right hemisphere is more important for nonverbal skills in men than women. Moreover, specialized tests of the relative dominance of the cerebral hemispheres suggest that girls attain left-hemisphere dominance (for language) a little ahead of boys.

Since some of the differences between males and females have a universality across culture and species, perhaps the sex-role standards promoted in our culture are neither arbitrary nor completely the product of what parents praise or punish. Each culture, in its wisdom, may promote those behaviors, talents, and motives that are easiest to establish in each of the sexes. However, biological differences between the sexes are subtle and have little or no implication for vocational roles in our society. There is every reason to believe that most of these roles, with the exception of the small number of jobs requiring great physical strength, can be filled by either sex.

Changes in Sex-Role Standards. Since the sex-role standards for men and women are currently different, the hierarchies of motives among men and women also vary. What is central for one sex is often peripheral for the other. In the recent past, most women wanted to be reassured of their ability to effect harmonious relations and to participate in reciprocal love relationships. These motives dominated their behavior with others. Although the same motives exist among men, they have been subordinated to the more pressing desire for power and a dominant position in interaction with others. However, the growing protest among women that these culturally arbitrary sex differences place the female in a subordinate role is producing profound changes in sex-role values. Contemporary women are more likely to assume an egalitarian relationship with a man in courtship and are less likely to be totally passive in a sexual context. Wives are insisting that husbands share equal responsibility for the infant and child. The division of labor, they argue, is unfair and unnatural. And many young men agree.

Clearly, the sex-role values that we have lived with for several hundred years are being transformed. Perhaps the known biological differences between the sexes can be totally overcome by culture, and the society can approach a state in which a person's sex is of no consequence for any significant role or activity except child-bearing and delivery. But we must ask if such a society will be satisfying to its members. Complementarity characterizes the most stable and gratifying relationships between people. The liberation of both women and men from the constraining stereotypes of the past may make it difficult for any heterosexual bond to remain strong for a reasonable period of time. There is a growing mutual understanding among young couples that each is capable of going it alone. The old-fashioned notion that man protected woman in return for the healing power of her love may have placed unjust burdens on both partners, but it allowed them to nurture the belief that they were necessary to each other. When both man and woman believe that their own self-actualization takes precedence over any pressure to salve the wounds of the other, potential commitments become fragile liaisons. A college senior, grappling with the uncertainty of his future, wrote to the young woman he loved:

> Can't you see I have to come to terms with myself? It's hard. I need you, need your concern, your love, your support. But you wouldn't answer. Now you are running away and leaving me to fight it alone. You could help me, but all you do is weigh me down. Help me, love me, make me feel I'm worth something.

The girl replied:

> I know you're having your hell, but how can I help, when I can't reach you? Besides I need you to help me. Don't bring me your hangups. I'm busy with my own. Can't you see I need my energy for me? (Goethals and Klos, p. 261.)

As men and women gradually develop the same profile of needs, total self-interest becomes a dangerous reality. Since separateness and isolation have never been preferred modes of living, we shall have to establish new bases for mutual dependence and need between the sexes. At present, however, each sex still has a different set of missions. Each still marches to a slightly different piper, sensitized to different facets of the same experience and gratified by what the other disregards.

We have now considered the major mechanisms of behavior change. Instruction, reinforcement, observation, and identification, acting alone or together, exert an enormous influence on every child. But these processes lose their power if the child is not motivated to display or adopt particular actions. Let us turn our attention therefore to human motives, their meaning, their developmental history, and how they influence behavior.

Motives

THE NATURE OF MOTIVES

Actions and thoughts are often directed at a goal, where a goal is simply a desired experience. A college senior enters the library after dinner; a ten-year-old teases his younger brother; a two-year-old carefully places a seventh block on a precarious tower of six. In all three cases, the person has some notion of a desired state of affairs—a goal. A motive is the mental representation of that goal. It is neither the action that gains the goal nor the feeling of excitement, tension, or distress that often accompanies the wish. Many children have thought of visiting Disneyland, yelling at their mother, or running away from home, but the motive was never acted upon and need not have been accompanied by a strong emotion. *The motive is simply the idea that stands for the desired experience.* Hence gratification, which is synonymous with the attainment of the goal, resembles the experience of finding a name that has been on the tip of one's tongue. Gratification is experiencing the match between the idea of the desired event and the event itself.

The reason we need a concept like "motive" to understand human functioning is that some of our actions are influenced by anticipations of the future. We need a concept to explain why a woman sitting in a quiet library suddenly rises from her chair, leaves the room, and returns after making a telephone call to arrange an after-dinner appointment. A representation of a future event provoked the action. If there is no internal physiological need or external pressure for the change in behavior, the cause is likely to be in the person's mind. When that cause is the idea of a future goal, the person is motivated. Unfortunately, a description of a person's actual behavior does not help us to understand its aim. The statement "John did not take the final exam" is too divorced from John's history to be of much value in understanding why John was absent for the test or in predicting John's behavior the next time a final exam is scheduled. No action, no matter how exact its description, contains enough information to allow us to infer its intention.

Motivated Versus Nonmotivated Behavior. Not all behaviors are motivated. Many actions are simply reactions to the pressures of the immediate situation. A person sits quietly in a concert hall because that is the expected posture. He may have been motivated when he initially purchased a ticket for the concert, but his "act of sitting quietly" in the auditorium is controlled by the situation. A person's behavior should be viewed as composed of paragraphs. The first action, like the first sentence of a new paragraph, is often generated from within. But the initial action places a serious restriction on the next one, just as a topic sentence sets constraints on the sentences that follow. If we could tell when a person was beginning a new paragraph in his behavior, in contrast to when he was merely acting in the middle of one, we might be better able to understand his motives.

The social scientist's view of human nature has been strongly influenced by the nineteenth-century assumption held by physical scientists that every event in nature has a cause. For most of this century psychologists believed that their task was to find the causes of behavior. Sigmund Freud made this theme essential in his psychoanalytical theory of man. The basic human motives, which Freud called the id impulses, were regarded as the causes of behavior and neurotic symptoms. A person's motives were not always obvious to either himself or an observer, but there had to be a motive for all behavior.

Current conceptions of human behavior are not so uncritically wedded to the idea that all action derives from motives. This is not equivalent, however, to saying that an action has no cause. Actions like sneezing and coughing are the product of unlearned, automatic reflexes. These behaviors are caused, but not by motives. Other actions are prompted by biological drives like hunger, thirst, pain, and the need for sleep. Still others are habits associated with subtle feeling states. For example, a professor talking to a group of students suddenly rises from his chair and walks around the room for a few moments. It is neither necessary nor reasonable to assume that he wanted to stand up, that there was a specific goal he wished to attain. Most likely, the professor stood up because this action had become a habitual response to a certain quality of excitement he experienced. Similarly, a four-month-old infant will babble in response to a smiling face. The infant does not want to babble, nor is he necessarily gratified by this noisemaking.

The most common examples of nonmotivated behavior are learned reactions to particular situations. An American child sits in a chair to eat, a Japanese child kneels on a pillow, an international traveler in an airport stands at a lunch counter. The specific posture of sitting, kneeling, or standing is appropriate to the context in which the person is dining. A chair invites sitting, a pillow invites kneeling, a counter invites standing. The reader may reply that it is not the specific posture displayed that is motivated but the act of eating. Yet we know that a person often eats breakfast at 8 A.M., lunch at noon, and dinner at 7 P.M. not because he has any desire for food but because it is the appropriate time to eat. The context of the family seated at a table set with bacon and eggs at 8 A.M. calls for the act of sitting down for breakfast. Thus many actions are learned routines to particular contexts and not necessarily the product of a motive.

Awareness of Motives. Although a motive is an idea about a goal, it is not always fully conscious and well defined. It is typically not the state we experience when we instruct ourselves, "I must go to the post office, then to the barber, and be back at the office by 1:30." A motive can be a verbalized reminder, a fleeting image, or a fragmented version of either. We must distinguish, moreover, between the latent representation of the goal, or the motive, and the activation of that idea, which is called *motivation*. A motivational state is best viewed as an abstract mental set, where a mental set can be likened to the tuning of a radio or television. When the dial is moved to a particular setting, the amplifier becomes maximally receptive to one set of signals and minimally receptive to all others. Similarly, when a person sits down to watch a news broadcast or a replay of a Gary Cooper movie, he readies himself to receive certain sounds and sights; he is mentally preparing for a particular set of events. This preparation is the state called motivation.

A motive that is activated limits perception as well as action, for it acts like a governor on a motor or a program in a computer. The mind can be likened to a large collection of routines with an executive deciding which routine should be activated. The motive instructs the executive to focus more selectively on one set of routines and to ignore others. A simple illustration of the meaning of motivation as a set can be seen in the behavior of a man driving home after a day at work. The man leaves his office at 6 P.M., reminding himself briefly of where he is going. This self-instruction takes less than a second. His mind then turns to other matters—the evening's work, the problems of the next day, the unsolved crises at the office. He gets into his car, starts the ignition, leaves the parking lot, and automatically makes the correct set of turns to his house without ever thinking about his actions or about the goal toward which he is driving. Had he decided as he left the office that he was going to a restaurant on the opposite side of the city, he would have made a different set of correct turns and also arrived at his goal. There was a brief moment when a representation of a goal led the man to select a set of action routines that ran off automatically. The motive was the brief representation of the goal.

Each person possesses hundreds of thousands of representations of goals, most of which lie dormant in the shadow of unawareness. Some representations are capable of being activated into consciously experienced wishes. Others are less available to awareness, a fact that led Freud to invent the notion of *unconscious motives*. A motive is said to be unconscious when a person is unaware of a set of goals that he desires. But ideas may be partially conscious for brief periods of time, and it is possible for a person to experience only fragments of a wish.

Moreover, a person does not have to recognize the significance of his motives in order to act on them. The young child who performs poorly in school does not say to himself, "I hate my mother and want her to be unhappy; therefore, I will fail in school." The child might have a fleeting awareness of his mother crying and believe that failure to comply with her wishes would cause her to become upset. If he has learned that she is distressed by poor grades, a certain group of behaviors will be selected, much as the representation of home in the driver's mind led him to select the correct set of turns to his house. When a child is aware of a motive, he knows the goal he wants. The child who takes on chores in order to obtain money to purchase a bicycle can tell us why he is working after school. But if possession of the bicycle was a way of evoking his older brother's jealousy, by obtaining a prize the brother did not have, the boy would probably not be able to tell us about this wish. Although the child seems unaware of his desire to antagonize his brother, he may have had a fleeting idea of his brother's angry face. He does not label this brief bit of knowledge as meanness or hostility (psychologists do that), but its existence defines the motive. Unfortunately, we do not know how to detect these fragile, wishladen representations. Since the child cannot verbalize them, we say that the motive is unconscious. But a fragmentary thought can be sufficient to activate a person toward attainment of a relevant goal.

An unconscious motive defines one end of a continuum of accessibility. At one extreme there is no awareness of a representation of a goal toward which a set of actions may be progressing. Thus the three-year-old, who is not aware of the rules of grammar, produces surprisingly correct sentences. We do not understand how a mental set can guide and order a group of complex behaviors. It is possible that the same factors that govern the relation between possession of rules of grammar and correct speech also apply to the relation between unconscious motives and behavior. For the selection of an action to gratify a motive is similar to the selection of a phrase for a sentence, or indeed a rule to solve a problem. A person possesses an abstract representation of a goal to be reached and, mysteriously, selects the right routine. In this sense, motivated behavior may be similar to the mental processes characteristic of all problem-solving. The essential ingredients are a representation of a goal and a set of strategies that might attain it.

Actions that seem to be obvious gratifications of one motive often turn out, upon analysis, to be gratifications of quite a different desire. Sometimes a person is fully aware of his desire for a certain goal but wishes to disguise it. He initiates behaviors that seem to be aimed at one goal, but his actions are intended for another. For example, a child wants to play with a toy another child possesses and offers the privileged one a substitute in the hope that he will attain the toy he wants. His clever bartering appears on the surface to be motivated by charitable impulses. On other occasions a person may believe that the goal-directed behavior he is engaging in is relevant to a conscious motive, but a primary motive, of which he is less aware, is the more significant cause of his action. For example, a college student emigrates to Canada to avoid the draft in the belief that he is motivated by a revulsion for the war in Vietnam. It is possible, however, that his action is motivated by a desire to avoid a situation in which, as a soldier, he might lose control of himself. The student may be afraid that he would behave irrationally if an officer issued an arbitrary order. This uncertainty frightens him and he emigrates, unaware of the influence of the second motive. Similarly, the student-protest movements attract some young adults whose desire for power is salient. Their campus behavior is in the service of this motive, although they believe it is aimed at less narcissistic goals.

Some of the most poignant examples of the mismatch of motives and behavior are seen in the crises of middle age and the ideological confusion of adults. The disillusionment of many Western adults comes from a recognition that longstanding actions have been directed at goals that have suddenly become unattractive. When the motives become accessible and the relation of behavior to wish becomes clear, the person recognizes that the things he has been doing for ten years have not been leading to the goals he really wants.

Degree of Elaboration of Motives. Psychologists have traditionally described the quantitative dimension of a motive in terms of *strength,* as a predisposition to behave. But a mental representation of warm, blue-green surf does not have strength the way the blow of a hand does. Motives, like all ideas, are best described not as varying in strength but in *degree of elaboration* and *capacity to crowd out other motives*. The degree of elaboration of a motive depends on the number of different representations of a goal that can serve the motive. Consider a six-year-old who wants more attention from his mother. If the representations of that goal include a variety of well-defined reactions from the mother—kissing, playing, verbal teasing, a present, a pat on the head—the motive is highly elaborated. If there are few representations of the goal, the motive is poorly elaborated.

The degree of elaboration of a motive increases with age, for the acquisition of language, introspection, and the honing of wishes in the frustrating world of action all sharpen and amplify the representation of goals. One corollary of this developmental change is that the older the child becomes, the greater the substitutability of his goals. A two-year-old who wants attention from his mother will tolerate fewer kinds of maternal reactions than will the older child, who is likely to accept many different forms of attention. The five-year-old with a desire for power has limited ways to gratify it; the adult's power motive can be gratified by wealth, perfection of a valued skill, or identification with a group or person possessing this resource. A motive becomes elaborated as its goal states become more diversified. Adults, however, do possess some poorly elaborated motives. An uncomfortable restlessness and confusion of purpose are prevalent conditions in contemporary Western society. Many adults wonder about how they should conduct their lives, a state that has produced a poorly elaborated motive to "know oneself" and a spate of cartoons illustrating men climbing mountains to ask wrinkled gurus, "What do I want?"

The Motive Hierarchy. A person's motives, like all his ideas, exist in a hierarchy, and each can be dominant at different times. The notion of position in a hierarchy comes closest to the popular term "preoccupation." There are times when we become so concerned with a particular goal that it is impossible to suppress it. Even if we are successful in replacing it with another thought for a few moments, we soon find it has pushed the temporary visitor aside and reinstated itself in the front of consciousness.

32

Motives high in the hierarchy at a given time push a person to relate his immediate experience to the motive and to seek out experiences that are likely to be gratifying. Consider the consequences of different hierarchies of motives for two adolescent boys at a party. The motive for a sexual encounter is ascendant for one; the motive to attract the attention of the group is ascendant for the other. Each will be watching different people, have different thoughts during the evening, and react with different amounts of joy or anguish when the lights go out.

Motives change their position in the hierarchy if they are continually frustrated. A child who is always disappointed in his attempts to gain the affection of his parents may turn his attention to gratifying hostility toward peers. He now becomes preoccupied with hurting others, and the motive for parental affection becomes subordinate to the motive of hostility. Usually, only a few motives dominate thought at a given time, for it is difficult to set the switches of attention in many directions at once.

Although man is motivated for a large number of different goals, ranging from political fame to monastic withdrawal from society, there are four primary motives that seem to be the basis for a great many secondary ones. These four motives—resolution of uncertainty, mastery, hostility, and sexuality—play an important role in helping us to understand the child's behavior in school. Let us now consider each of these motives in turn, devoting special attention to their relevance to the tasks of education.

THE MOTIVE TO RESOLVE UNCERTAINTY

One of man's primary motives is to resolve the uncertainty that is generated when he encounters deviations from his conception of the truth. People continually carve from the flux of experience ideas of what they believe to be the essential nature of the world. The child as well as the adult constructs representations of what he sees, hears, touches, and smells. These representations are the mind's way of coding reality. It takes only about ten weeks for an infant to create a representation of a human face, and once he does so he puts great faith in the essential correctness of that idea. Man is disposed to believe that "what is, ought to be." Whenever an experience

33

disturbs his understanding of what ought to be, he is motivated to confront that disturbance and resolve it.

Sources of Uncertainty. The earliest source of uncertainty is the unfamiliar, where unfamiliarity implies a discrepancy between a mental representation of an aspect of experience and a specific event that is both similar to and different from the representation. The discrepant event can occur in the outside world—a strange animal or a friend's failure to smile; or it can originate within the body—an odd feeling in the chest or an intermittent throbbing in the forearm. These events alert the individual and generate uncertainty. If the unfamiliar experience cannot be explained or dealt with, fear or anxiety is likely to follow.

Once a mental representation of an object or event is established—for example, a young child's representation of "mother"—all other events in the world are seen as either related or unrelated to that idea. Most objects—a fish, a bottle, a tree—bear no relation to the original representation. A much smaller set of events—another woman, for example—is closely related. All variations of the mother are also obviously related to the original representation. If the child's mother were to change her hairstyle, wear an unusual dress, or acquire a scar, she would become a discrepant stimulus for him. Some of the features of the mother remain the same; others are different. These discrepancies attract the child's attention and alert him, as though the trigger of a gun had been cocked. The child is now in a special state of tension, or uncertainty, and something must happen. The child must be able to understand the discrepancy, act upon it, change it, or remove it. If the child can do any of these things quickly, within a few seconds, the state of alert tension disappears and no strong emotion follows. However, if the child cannot cope with the discrepancy, fear emerges and maintains the motivation to resolve the uncertainty and reduce the uncomfortable feelings of fear. The specific strategies initiated to cope with the discrepancy and alleviate the fear will depend on the child's unique history.

A second source of uncertainty is inconsistency between two ideas or between an idea and behavior. For example, a child who believes in God may be told by a friend that such an idea is silly. Or a child who believes his father to be wise and good may overhear a relative criticize the father's virtue. In each case, the child has two inconsistent beliefs and is uncertain as to which deserves credence; he cannot hold both and must do something to resolve the uncertainty. Two ideas claim the same degree of legitimacy, and the child must decide which one is the fraud. The conflict is usually resolved either by changing each idea a little, and accepting both as partially valid, or by rejecting one of the beliefs as untrue. Occasionally, the child will resolve the conflict simply by ignoring the inconsistency.

Inconsistency between a belief and behavior also generates uncertainty. A child feels he is honest, yet he has just told a lie. He believes he is brave, but he has just crossed the street to avoid running into a bully. His actions cast doubt on his beliefs about himself, and uncertainty follows. If the child cannot resolve the uncertainty, perhaps by rationalizing the inconsistency in some way, he will become emotionally upset. Depending on the nature of the inconsistency, he will experience anxiety, shame, or guilt. Man's dislike of inconsistency between his beliefs and behavior pushes him to invent rational bases for his actions, for if one irrational action is permitted expression, no matter how benevolent its effects, there is the danger that thousands of other irrational acts will demand equal recognition. And there will be no way to decide which ones are entitled to public display. Man likes to believe he acts out of rationality, and he continually arranges his world to make this possible.

A third source of uncertainty is the inability to predict the future, especially if the doubt hovers over potentially unpleasant events like punishment, physical harm, failure, or rejection. When a person is unable to predict the future—when he does not know what events will occur—he cannot know what behaviors and mental sets to activate in preparation for the future events. As a result, potentially incompatible tendencies are activated. To be unsure of the future affection of another is to entertain simultaneously the contradictory beliefs "She loves me—she loves me not."

Uncertainty over when psychological catastrophe will strike is one of man's most discomforting states. If he cannot ignore the doubt or reassure himself, fear or anxiety will mount, often to an intensity that prevents him from initiating any productive action or idea, and he will be driven to resolve the uncertainty. An observation of a two-year-old boy is illustrative. The boy had put some freshly laundered linen into a toilet bowl. When his mother discovered what he had done she lost her temper and hit the child severely, perhaps more harshly than she intended. The boy was obviously surprised, frightened, and in pain, and he cried hard for several minutes. It was a traumatic experience. The next day the boy found another pile of freshly laundered linen and again put it into the toilet bowl. He then walked into the kitchen where his mother was drinking coffee, stiffened his body to prepare for a spanking, and announced what he had done. His behavior in this situation was clearly not an act of revenge for yesterday's spanking. If it had been, the child would not have told his mother and prepared for punishment. The boy had been frightened by the unpredictably severe spanking he had received and needed to reduce the uncertainty. He had to attain control; he had to know when the knife was going to fall. So he committed the crime again and presented himself for justice. But on the second day *he* was controlling the time and location of the punishment. It was more important for him to reduce the uncertainty about the consequences of future play with laundry than to avoid a painful spanking. As we might expect, after this second punishment the child stopped dropping laundry in the toilet. He had gained the needed information.

The two-year-old pulls on curtains, brings a lamp into the kitchen, entangles himself in his mother's knitting, or plays with newly ironed napkins. The child's mother often regards this behavior as mischievous, and psychologists have on occasion called it aggressive. But these acts are not always impelled by hostile motives toward the mother. They may be the child's way of finding out what is right and wrong, of discovering how he can get his mother to respond to him, or of learning how to interact with his mother when he has violated a rule. The mischievous behavior is an attempt to obtain some information about the rules of living. A young child typically glances at his mother when he is about to commit an act whose legitimacy is questionable, whether it is touching a strange vase, taking a bite of a freshly baked cake, or teasing a baby sister. The child wants to know if what he is about to do is permissible. At the last moment, just before the action, the uncertainty mounts high enough to force him to make a response.

Uncertainty over the presence of the parent is particularly salient for young children; hence "school phobia" is a common problem among six-year-olds. The child who suddenly develops a fear of going to school is usually afraid not of *school* but of *leaving home*. The child is not certain that his mother will be home when he returns from school. Children test limits with adults in order to find out what is permitted; they want to know the rules of each game, contest, or interaction so that they can more securely select future actions. Once the child knows what is right and wrong, he will try to match his behavior to that standard in order to keep uncertainty controlled.

Reactions to Uncertainty. Although uncertainty often generates unpleasant feelings of fear, anxiety, or guilt, it does so only when a person cannot interpret, modify, or act upon it. It is the inability to cope with uncertainty that produces the distress and subsequent attempts to attain goals that will provide some control. Many of the popular motives ascribed to people by psychologists or novelists are derivative of the primary motive to resolve uncertainty and its subsequent anguish. If a person can act upon the initial discrepancy or inconsistency—if he can interpret, ignore, or modify it—the uncertainty will be alleviated. This resolution of uncertainty and aborting of distress can be seen in many situations. If a ten-month-old infant is placed in a strange room alone, he typically cries. But if the infant crawls into the strange room from an adjoining room where his mother is sitting, he will not cry. He looks around, becomes alerted, and crawls back through the open door to his mother. Objectively, the situation in the strange room is the same. But in the first instance there was nothing the child could do in the unusual environment. In the second instance the infant had an effective action to perform when he was alerted by the discrepancy; he could crawl back through the door to his mother. This action blocked the fear.

Similarly, a one-year-old who watches his mother walk away from him in a strange room will not cry if his attention is absorbed in an activity. If he is passive and doing nothing, he will cry. Uncertainty leads to fear only when there are no available reactions to cope with it or to detract attention from it. These simple observations of the infant's behavior reveal an essential principle about anxiety and its control. Man continually finds himself in unfamiliar rooms, but whether he is seized by fear or provoked to make a constructive defense against the uncertain depends on whether he sees an open door and believes he can reach that exit in a reasonable time.

Uncertainty is not always accompanied by unpleasant feelings of anxiety. On many occasions it is followed by a subtle and pleasant emotion that invites the label *excitement*. The critical factors that determine whether excitement or anxiety will follow uncertainty are, first, whether a person has responses available to deal with the uncertainty and, second, whether the uncertainty is self-generated or imposed from without. Anxiety occurs when the uncertainty is imposed on the individual and he has no reaction to cope with it. Excitement occurs when the person generates the uncertainty and possesses an action that can resolve it.

This distinction between uncertainty generated by the individual and uncertainty imposed from without has important implications. Dogs become helpless in a simple problem situation in which they experience a series of electric shocks that they initially cannot turn off, no matter what they do. They eventually become passive in this situation. When they are tested later, under conditions in which they can act to avoid the painful shocks, they continue to lie helplessly. Apparently the dogs learned that there was nothing they could do and hence did not try to solve the problem. (Seligman and Maier, 1967.)

The uncertainty that accompanies excitement arises from a person's estimate of the potential effectiveness of a set of responses aimed at a goal. The uncertainty that accompanies anxiety results from the absence of any responses to deal with a discrepancy. *A person seeks uncertainty when he can deal with it; he avoids uncertainty when he cannot deal with it.* Thus we do not deny the obvious fact that man seeks challenge and fresh experiences. At first blush, this may seem to negate the view that the control of uncertainty is a primary motive. But man seeks adventure and new ideas only when he believes he has a set of actions and ideas appropriate to the challenge. He rarely seeks the novel when he does not believe he can handle it. The occurrence of anxiety or excitement hangs delicately on the availability of actions and thoughts to cope with the uncertain event. Man seeks this brand of uncertainty because he enjoys taming it.

The most extreme form of protection against uncertainty can be seen in the behavior of the schizophrenic. The schizophrenic patient is seriously withdrawn from others and frightened of physical or psychological contact with them. Every action announces his terror of relating to another person. When he is willing to talk about his feelings, we learn that he has split his physical body from his psychological self. He does not perceive what we call the "I" to be a part of his face, limbs, or trunk. And his speech is punctuated with irrational and often incomprehensible phrases. The schizophrenic might reply to the gentle question "How are you feeling today?" with a cryptic, "Feeling, speeling; oranges and pie; I cut you a piece to help you live."

The psychiatrist R. D. Laing has suggested that these symptoms can be understood as an extreme reaction to the most profound sources of uncertainty any human being can experience. The schizophrenic is afraid both of being destroyed by others and of destroying them. He desires neither. His sense of self is so fragile that he lives with the continual fear that if anyone comes near him he will lose whatever remnant of an identity he still holds. If someone were to show him the slightest kindness he is sure he would psychologically dissolve into the nurturant person and be engulfed by the giver. Since he regards himself as evil, he is afraid that if he enters into any relationship he will hurt or destroy the other person. The schizophrenic speaks illogically in order to avoid being understood; for to be understood is to be known, and this may tempt another to come closer. His "crazy" talk is functional, for it keeps others away.

The schizophrenic's fears are so overwhelming and his uncertainty so profound that his only protection against them is to deny that the self exists. He may kill himself so that no one else can do it first. The dramatic defense of the schizophrenic bears some resemblance to the boy who dropped the laundry into the toilet and announced his crime. The child, like the schizophrenic, placed himself in control, even though the cost in terms of psychic pain was enormous.

The fact that other people are a greater source of uncertainty for modern man than the physical environment has led to an elaboration of motives surrounding people. It is perhaps not surprising that over the last four thousand years there has been a growing tendency to regard people, rather than demons, spirits, poisons, herbs, or bodily humors, as the primary cause of mental illness. Thus modern psychiatrists believe that a mother's treatment of her child or the social conditions in a city are critical determinants of childhood violence or adult schizophrenia, whereas ancient Greek or medieval physicians placed the blame for these afflictions on impersonal, demonic, or biological forces.

Secondary Motives. Each of these sources of uncertainty—discrepancy, inconsistency, and unpredictability—leads to the primary motive to resolve it in some way. There are many ways to accomplish this goal, and they vary with age, culture, and personal history. Some children learn that staying close to a parent alleviates uncertainty; such children are called dependent. Others try to get praise for a painting, a report card, or a clean room; these children are said to seek attention and recognition. The wish to dominate can also be motivated by uncertainty. When a child feels he is subordinate to another, he can never be sure when the dominant one will place demands on him or coerce him into performing some action. The subordinate role always contains more uncertainty than the dominant one. Hence most people want to assume a dominant position with others.

Wishes for praise, dominance, or closeness to others—and their accompanying actions—that result from the primary motive to resolve uncertainty are called *secondary motives*. Since most adults are capable of helping the child reduce uncertainty, children usually want a close, reassuring relationship with them. But some children learn to withdraw from adults when they are anxious and uncertain because they have not had the experience of having adults help them control uncertainty and fear, or because they are not sure how adults will treat them.

Absorption in an activity is another way to alleviate uncertainty. In an ingenious experiment, monkeys were taught to press a lever to avoid painful electric shocks. When the experimenter subsequently eliminated the shocks for long periods of time, the monkeys pressed the lever more often than when the shocks were present. That is, when shock became an uncertain event, they used the response that was most effective in the past—pressing the lever. (Stretch *et al.*, 1968.) An action directed at a goal diverts the mind and aborts the discomfort of apprehension. Our belief in the therapeutic value of work is based on this idea.

This principle also helps us to understand the behavior of teachers and administrators who have been made uneasy by the critical attitude of both parents and press toward the school's practices and apparent failures. Educators are anxious because they are not sure what they should do. This anxiety has led them to become preoccupied with change in any form as a way of buffering the uneasiness.

Many school systems eagerly await the announcement of any new curriculum, and a great deal of busywork follows. The new curriculum keeps teachers, principals, and supervisors occupied. They are doing something, and this activity keeps anxiety muted. As might be expected, many teachers and administrators have developed a motive for devising new curricula. For the act of constructing, perfecting, implementing, evaluating, and finally discarding curricula dilutes uncertainty and becomes an attractive goal in its own right.

The young teacher may be anxious about the poor progress of her pupils, the noise in the room, the unruly boy in the back row. She is prone to leap at simple solutions. Drill work, ordering children to the office, and trying a new reading program seem to be the answer to her troubles. The teacher busies herself with mastery of the program and introduces it into her classroom. The involvement in the curriculum diverts her attention from her uncertainty and anxiety and she feels better about her work. If her anxiety remains low, she will seek out new educational procedures regularly whenever she feels uneasy. In time she will develop a motive for this activity.

This is not to imply that curriculum changes are of no value. New curricula are helpful and, if successful, will make educators more willing to try new ideas. Moreover, even if a new curriculum is not superior to an older one, the emotional involvement in finding and mastering it alleviates the teacher's uncertainty and she will view it as beneficial. Who is to say it is not?

The child's love of play is not unlike the teacher's devotion to devising or changing curricula. Young children do not like to sit and think. They actively seek variety in experience and through games. Although there is as much uncertainty in the child's world as in the world of the adult, the adult has a richer store of knowledge that he can use to analyze his doubts and reassure himself. The child is less able to use this defense of intellectual analysis and therefore chooses play, which can be so totally absorbing that it effectively prevents him from dwelling too long on uncomfortable uncertainties. During the long work periods in school the child is confronted with many sources of uncertainty. But he knows that afternoon games, with their fixed rules, are only a few hours away, and he is eager to begin them.

The varied schools of psychotherapy offer another example of the way in which involvement in an activity can alleviate anxiety.

Each school of therapy seems to be effective with particular symptoms and patients. Yet the means by which each method attains its results are dramatically different. Consider the treatment of a woman who is afraid of crowds. Every time she is in a crowd her heart beats fast, her breathing becomes short, her palms sweat profusely, and she feels terrified. If she sees a psychoanalyst, he may tell her, after a certain number of sessions, that she is afraid of suddenly losing control of herself and undressing in public. He reassures her that she can control these impulses and that there is nothing to fear and suggests that she tell herself this the next time she is in a crowd. The woman believes the doctor's interpretation, for it matches her current understanding of her personality and her theory of mental life. The next time she is in a crowd and senses anxiety mounting, she is reminded of the analyst's interpretation. She thinks about it and reassures herself that she is capable of inhibiting her urge to undress in public. As she becomes engrossed in these thoughts her anxiety diminishes. "Thinking about the interpretation" recruits her attention, and her fear is reduced. The woman feels better and both doctor and patient are convinced of the validity of the explanation that produced the cure.

The same woman might have made an appointment with a modern behavior therapist, rather than with the psychoanalyst. This doctor tells her that her fears are conditioned reactions to crowds. It is not necessary to know why the fears originally developed; it is essential only to break the conditioned habit, to decondition her. The doctor tells the woman that this deconditioning can be accomplished by learning to relax when one is in a fearful state. The feeling of relaxation will become conditioned to the sight of the crowd, and the fear will be extinguished. The doctor suggests that one way to become more relaxed is by controlling one's breathing, and he tutors the patient in the breathing exercises to be used when she is afraid. The woman believes the therapist's prescription, for his suggestion matches her theoretical understanding of the cause of her symptoms. The next time she is in a crowd and feels fear rising, she reminds herself of the doctor's suggestion and begins to concentrate on her breathing. As her attention becomes recruited to the task of relaxing, her fear recedes. The anxiety yields as she concentrates on her breathing.

The essential similarity between these two therapy procedures is that the patient believed in the effectiveness of an engrossing action or thought sequence and implemented it. The action required concentration and made it difficult to dwell on the feelings of anxiety. Thus it is possible that the fundamental basis for the cure in each case was not the specific nature of the therapy but the fact that the woman implemented a routine that she believed would help her.* The therapist might have told the woman to think of God, read the Bible, have a child, fall in love, take a Caribbean vacation, or work for civil rights. If the woman believed in the rationale behind any of these suggestions—that is, if she believed that the actions would allay her fear—and if she trusted the doctor and followed his suggestions, her anxiety would probably diminish.

Study of the enormous variety of "therapeutic" procedures used in different societies suggests that the essential curative agent in psychotherapy is the resolution of uncertainty through the provision of rituals that engage the patient's faith. Members of a mountainous Peruvian community believe that if a person, with the help of a healer, can display courage while hallucinating that a boa constrictor is entering his body, he must be emotionally strong enough to recover from his psychological symptoms. Among the Yoruba of Nigeria the healer—called the *babalawo*—functions very much like an American psychiatrist. He explains each illness and suggests remedies by relating the symptoms to folktales and myths, rather than to early childhood trauma, as we do in the United States. The healer may tell a patient that he has developed certain symptoms because he was destined to be a diviner but failed to assume his responsibility. He can be cured if he becomes initiated into the cult of diviners. This initiation totally involves the patient's energies, for he must memorize long sections of folktales and poetry. (Prince, 1968.) In modern Japan a new form of psychotherapy, called Morita therapy, is gaining adherents. The curative regime consists of a brief initial period of enforced rest followed by work. The patient is told that he should evaluate himself by the products of his work rather than by his symptoms. (Iwai and Reynolds, 1970.)

* Professor S. Valins has demonstrated that a woman who believed that her heart rate did not change while she looked at pictures of dangerous snakes subsequently showed less fear to a live snake. Presumably the subject's conclusion that she was not afraid stemmed from her belief that a steady heartbeat means low fear; however, the evidence for the steady heartbeat was coming not from her own body but from a tape recorder.

In each of these therapeutic procedures—which seem to be equally effective—the patient implements an ideology and a set of behaviors that he believes will help him. Since all cultures differ in their local theories of mental illness, the specific therapeutic regimes they select also differ. But in every case the curative value of the therapy seems to be based on the same basic processes—the adoption of a coherent set of ideas and the implementation of a set of actions that the patient believes will resolve his psychic distress.

The social institutions of most societies are conveniently organized procedures to provide action routines to cope with uncertainty. In our society, marriage, work, and school provide complex, ritualized involvements that bind our attention and turn us away from preoccupation with the daily discrepancies, inconsistencies, and doubts that cannot be easily interpreted or acted upon. Similarly, sexual behavior is often used unconsciously to resolve uncertainty, for an affair can be as totally absorbing an enterprise as work, investing in the stock market, yachting, or caring for three young children. Each of these routines fills the vitally human need for absorption in an activity with manageable uncertainty. A college sophomore captured this delicate tension: "I am afraid to stop studying or going to class, for these rituals keep me from the terror of saying, 'The hell with it all.' . . . Then where would I be? I'm scared of not believing in anything."

The Failure of Traditional Solutions. Many of our traditional methods of dealing with uncertainty are failing because a large portion of the population has stopped believing in their effectiveness. Young people are confronted with the discrepant experience of knowing large numbers of people to whom they feel similar but with whom they do not share beliefs about the rituals that heal. This inconsistency is toxic to the effectiveness of an ideology or behavioral routine. Hence some high school and college students are caught in a strangling web of apathy. They are confronted with all three sources of uncertainty—an unpredictable future, bizarre headlines, and doubt about the simple truths they have heard from their parents. But they have no effective set of ideas or actions to deal with these puzzles.

Youth's indifference to the traditional goals embodied in school and work is growing at what the adult generation regards as an alarming rate. There are several reasons for this disaffection with older values. The belief that science and technology have brought more destruction and pollution than benefit has soured many potential professional careers. And there is no reason for a student to work for *A*'s in his courses if he has decided to ignore graduate school—or if he is ambivalent about it and anticipates feeling no pain upon a rejected application. The swelling egalitarianism in our society slices at the motivations for status and power that have always been a force for work. If prestige is empty and elitism wicked, it is easy to forget about grades, for students of every age view the grade as a good-conduct medal to be used in parades or to gain entry into hallowed halls, rather than as a confidential report on the state of their expertise. Grades are losing their legitimacy and young people are finding it increasingly difficult to rationalize working for them.

There has always been strong peer pressure against overzealousness in studies because it suggests childish conformity to the teacher. But this basis for resistance has been joined by a catechism that holds academic work to be irrelevant when placed alongside the moral crises of society. Investment of affect in school is *prima facie* evidence of lack of concern for the relevant issues of the day.

We come now to the essence of the problem. If young people had another goal to replace school and career there would be less alarm, for there would be no apathy. But they do not; the young are searching for an effective substitute. Several candidates are gaining popularity on high school and college campuses. The wish to test the depth and strength of one's emotional capacities has become one alternative. The easy availability of drugs has made this contest exciting and worth entering. Many young people ask themselves a question earlier generations never thought of: "How much pounding and expansion can my emotional shield accept?" The motive to master this challenge is likely to expend itself in a short while, for the total intensity and variety of experience is soon exhausted, the answer to the original question is clear, and the uncertainty is resolved. One will have learned how tough or fragile the inner self is. Moreover, drugs do not enable the student to escape the irrevocable truth that he cannot live only in the present; he must create dreams. During an LSD trip one college student wrote:

> Even during the darkest moments of the experience I must have held on to the hope that out of the chaos some fragment of worth might be retained. I have often thought that if this hope had not been present I would have surrendered myself

45

and probably never would have recovered. We all must hold on to something, even if it is unpleasant. (Goethals and Klos, p. 146.)

A second goal gaining advocates is the search for honesty and intimacy in human encounters. Any ritual that carries the flimsiest decoration of artificiality is shunned, for it prevents contact and dehumanizes by forcing unnatural roles on unwilling actors who do not like the game of pretend. This ethic is more viable, for it is profoundly human. Since it is, in the extreme, unattainable, it is forever laced with some uncertainty and therefore satisfies the main requirement for permanence. Fortunately, it is a more healing motive than the individualistic competitiveness that captured the energy of earlier generations. If our society can nurture this freshly born objective, our twenty million young adults may be able to find a more comfortable and involving morality that will be toxic to the infectious boredom being carried into our institutional structures each day.

When man is motivated to resolve uncertainty, he is not deprived of a state called certainty, in the same sense that he is deprived of warmth when cold or water when thirsty. Psychological uncertainty is characterized by a particular organization of ideas and is accompanied by a physiological state of "alertness." This state has an inherent lability and is usually followed by the activation of mental processes that produce a different organization of ideas and a dissolution of the alerted state. The new arrangement is neither a reduction nor an attenuation of the first, but a different set of ideas. Some people may feel that the phrase "resolving uncertainty" is defensive, that it implies that man dislikes the unknown and avoids new challenges. At the moment, the choice of words is a matter of taste. Given the sparsity of data on this issue, "the motive to know" might just as well be substituted for "the motive to resolve uncertainty." Although the first phrase is more flattering to man than the second, the logic and implications of the argument seem to this writer to be almost identical.

THE MOTIVE FOR MASTERY

The motive for mastery—the wish to enhance one's knowledge, skill, or talent—is related to the motive to resolve uncertainty. There are, however, two major differences. First, the mastery motive is activated when a person generates a discrepancy between his level of accomplishment and the level to which he aspires. Uncertainty occurs when another person or event imposes a discrepancy between what the person believes to be true and reality. Second, the mastery motive does not always have a distinct alerting state that precedes the wish. A four-year-old may see a pile of blocks in the corner of a room and quietly sit down and build an elaborate house. If we ask him to stop, he does not; if we try to make him stop, he becomes angry. He is deeply involved in what he is doing. But it is unlikely that the child experienced any strong tension as he walked to the blocks, or even as he began building the house.

The desire to perfect a skill, finish a task, or solve a challenging problem can, of course, arise as a secondary motive based on the wish to resolve uncertainty. For example, a child may work hard in school to avoid criticism from teachers or parents—that is, to resolve the uncertainty surrounding adult acceptance. An adolescent girl may strive for better grades to maintain her father's affection; an adolescent boy may perfect his ability to fight in order to become the leader of a gang. Mastery often serves as a secondary motive to gain acceptance, love, and power. Perhaps the purest expression of this dynamic is captured in a statement made by a young woman following the anguish of an abortion: "I wish I could be what everyone wants."

Sources of the Mastery Motive. Although the motive for mastery can arise as a secondary motive, it also has a set of primary foundations, which are based on three goals: the desire to match behavior to a standard, the desire to predict the environment, and the wish to define the self.

As noted earlier, the child is continually acquiring ideas about the world—how tall people are, how many feet cows have, how cold snow is, how fast cars travel. Once he decides on the true characteristics of these phenomena he comes to believe in his decisions and he tries hard to maintain them. A child builds up a storehouse of beliefs and expectations about how the world should be. Some of these rules about the world he has experienced directly. He knows that milk is white, that chairs are for sitting, that dogs bark. The child is also aware of other rules that he has not experienced. He has been told

47

that mountains have snow in the summer, that Hong Kong is a crowded city, that alligators have long snouts. These rules are like compasses that guide behavior and reasoning.

The child tries to simulate, by construction or imitation, some of these idealized states. The four-year-old builds a house of blocks because he has an idea of what such a house should look like and blocks are available. A man climbs a mountain because he has a representation of what it might look like from the top and there are mountains available. However, it is obviously fallacious to predict that any time a child sees some blocks he will stop and build a house. There has to be an additional element of *uncertainty about reaching the idealized state.* The child must have some doubt about his ability to match his actions to the ideal. If he is perfectly certain he can build a house of blocks, he will have no motivation to build it. Similarly, if he is perfectly certain he *cannot* build the house, he will not be motivated to try. The motive for mastery is generated only when the child is a little unsure. Hence one condition for activation of the mastery motive is possession of an idea about some idealized experience (called the *standard*) and some uncertainty about being able to match one's feelings, thoughts, or behaviors to that standard.

A second basis for the mastery motive is the desire to predict future events. Adults spend much of each day unconsciously estimating what the weather will be like, what the boss' attitude will be, how tired they will feel at 6 P.M., how much traffic they will encounter on the highway. The child too is caught up in the obsessiveness of prediction. He tries to predict what will happen in school, how his friends will behave toward him, how well he will do in the afternoon baseball game, how soon the recess bell will ring. The child wants to predict events accurately because it gives him a feeling of control over them, just as the boy who threw a pile of laundry into the toilet confessed to his mother in order to be able to predict when punishment would occur. Every person wants to be in control of events rather than a pawn; he wants to be able to anticipate when, where, or how unpleasant events will occur in order to prepare for them. This desire leads to many forms of mastery behavior. A man who invests in stocks may be testing his ability to predict the rise and fall of prices, and his behavior is driven as much by this motive as by a desire for increased wealth. The child spends much of his first two years in school trying to predict what will happen and how he will be evaluated. Once he is able to do this, usually by the fifth grade, his involvement in school tasks diminishes. He has figured out the tasks and wants to turn to more challenging enigmas.

A child's behavior with a new game is one of the best examples of how the desire to predict uncertain outcomes fuels mastery behavior. If the child is unable to predict his performance, he is likely to work harder at the game. Once he has mastered it, he can turn his attention to another activity. The behavior of an infant with a new toy provides another illustration. A one-year-old discovers a toy xylophone and begins to play it. It makes different sounds and he explores, clumsily and inefficiently perhaps, the pattern of sounds. He begins to grow tired of the toy when nothing new happens, when he has exhausted the possibilities and is surprised no more. Each man's life consists of a series of attempts to predict his reactions in uncertain contexts. When performance in one context becomes predictable, he moves on to another. The joy is in mastering the unknown challenge, in the activity rather than in the product.

Emotion is most intense when a person is gaining predictive control, not when it has been gained. A newly graduated physicist goes to work for an electronics firm. He gains knowledge and experience and eventually accepts the responsibility for building six plants. Finally, at age thirty-eight, with the six plants completed, he tells his boss that he is bored. The man became most apathetic at the moment when we would expect him to be experiencing maximal satisfaction because his involvement in his work derived from his desire to predict and control the many uncertain outcomes of his job. Although a motive for mastery is activated when a person tries to attain an outcome with some uncertainty, *he only picks uncertain goals for which he has a response to make.* Uncertainties that generate no appropriate action are usually followed by anxiety.

A third basis for the mastery motive is the desire for self-definition. Every person wants to know his outstanding characteristics, the traits that define the self-as-object to the self-as-person. This desire is the essential component of the wish to gain information about the self, to know who one is. A college student remembers thinking before his first experience with a drug, "If I did not subject myself to this experience at least once, I might be missing something potentially enlightening."

Since the specific information that is valued depends on the culture, the child will turn toward society to discover the characteristics he should master. Contemporary Western society celebrates the significance of "knowing yourself," and young adults seek life experiences that they hope will provide partial answers to this puzzling question. For many young people this motive even pushes sexuality to a secondary position. They postpone marriage or sever a sexually gratifying relationship because they believe it will interfere with their search for self-definition. One young woman explains why she allowed the man she loves to leave her:

> I guess I'm just at the point of feeling able to develop some of my other talents apart from the housewife and mother roles which I know so well and could so easily get completely sucked into. But I musn't stop now—I just now see myself as able to develop a significance of my own and I think I'm afraid that for awhile anyway marriage might divert my attention too much. . . . My primary purpose has been to understand myself, for if that task is not accomplished I fail to understand how I can be of value to anyone else. (Goethals and Klos, p. 181.)

Some questions about the self can be resolved without anyone else's help. But in most cases the only way to evaluate oneself is to be with others. The culture tells a girl she should be beautiful. But how can she know how attractive she is unless she is pursued by men she values and can compare herself with a wide range of women who define beauty? The social group decides who is attractive, seductive, plain, or homely. A young black woman writes:

> There is always the problem of the white woman and her standard of beauty. It is her world. She stares out of billboards and *Mademoiselle* with all the cool and self-possession of the adored. And we of long arms, liquid eyes, and full lips want to be acknowledged. . . . If only our [black] men would stop chasing the white quasi-goddess. We wait . . . and I know few girls who give a damn about the current beauty standards. Beauty is a state of mind. Black women are reaching for that state of mind. But beauty takes a man to tell you. . . . Any

woman needs a man to realize herself fully, sexually and emotionally. And the same is true of a man. (Goethals and Klos, p. 152.)

Gratification of the desire to know the self too often requires a comparison with others. Our infamous tests of intellectual ability—be they the Binet IQ or college board scores—present the student not with an absolute score but with a rating that tells him how well he performed in relation to all the other students who took the test that day. Perhaps psychological maturity should be defined as that time in life when a person has established such a well-articulated understanding of himself that he can decide on the quality or morality of an action without showing it to anyone or comparing it with the actions of others. A few fortunate adults come close to attaining this precious state; most do not. Children are clearly not capable of making completely independent evaluations of the degree to which they possess culturally valued attributes. Unfortunately, the child must use his friends to decide how big, strong, kind, attractive, smart, honest, or artistic he is. Since the child wants to know his assets and limitations, he is motivated to master difficult tasks in order to obtain some feedback on how well he is doing. The child wants an identity, and it is composed in part of his profile of talents. In order to develop a well-delineated positive identity he must master certain tasks. One of the critical factors in this process is the uniqueness of the skill to be mastered. There is minimal advantage in acquiring a talent that everyone possesses. The ability to walk, hold a fork, open a door, or make rhymes adds little to the self-definition. These skills enable the child to feel similar to others but they do not permit him to feel different from others. Thus the child is moved to acquire skills that other children do not have or to develop exceptional competence at an everyday skill. The representation to be attained is the perception of self as more competent than another. The more unique the profile of competences, the better delineated the self-concept.

IMPLICATIONS FOR THE TEACHER

Since the teacher is concerned with increasing the mastery motivation of her students, it is helpful to consider the implications of this discussion for classroom practices. The desire for mastery is ascendant in the motive hierarchy when three conditions are met: (1) the goal state to be achieved is clear; (2) the child possesses the responses that will enable him to attain the goal; and (3) the child is a little uncertain of his ability to attain the goal or to predict the outcome of his action. In short, the child must know what he wants to achieve, must know how to start the work, and must have a moderate expectancy of success. The school usually tries to change the child's mastery motivation by frightening him or coercing him, rather than by changing any of these three factors. Too often, the teacher sees her job as teaching facts—so many per day, month, or year. This goal is less important than convincing the child that, when faced with a difficult problem, he can call upon certain strategies to begin the work. The teacher must persuade the child that he possesses intellectual talents which, if used, can lead to success. She must teach him to expect success and must show him how to maximize his chances of succeeding. Lecturing the child about facts he does not know only awes him and tempts him to believe what he already feels too strongly—namely, that he does not know very much.

The teacher should institute exercises or games that involve estimation and guessing about phenomena with which the child is familiar. For example, the fifth-grade teacher might ask her students to guess how many generations of people it would take to get to the nearest star. The teacher could facilitate clever guesses by giving the class a general understanding of the meaning of a light year and of how many light years away the nearest star is. Similarly, the teacher might give her students current daily birth and death rate figures for the world and ask them to estimate when the world's population will be twice what it is today. An increased emphasis on puzzles and riddles that invite good guesses should benefit mastery motivation.

The teacher can play an important role in making each child aware of his special areas of competence. The primary-grade teacher should magnify the small differences that exist in the talents of her students. She might make an inventory of each child's profile of competences—including music, art, physical coordination, reading, writing, and arithmetic—as early in the school year as possible. The teacher should use this information to create work groups in which each child has one area of relatively superior skill, no matter how small the actual difference in competence. A boy who is only a trifle better in spelling than the other children in his work group will exaggerate the actual difference, for the mind typically transforms little differences into large ones. This principle can be seen in the phenomenon of Mach bands. If a set of concentric black and white circles of equal intensity is rotated at a fixed and fast speed, the eye will perceive the outer black band as darker and the outer white band as whiter than the black and white areas inside the figure. This effect, which has a sound neurological basis, is one instance of the more general principle that small contrasts are exaggerated by the mind.

People also seem to operate this way at a conceptual level. If we see a small-boned figure with short hair, slacks, and sneakers, we have to make a decision about whether it is male or female. If we decide it is female, we will react to the figure as completely as we would if she were wearing long hair, a skirt, and sandals. Language is primarily a set of symbols for discrete categories. We have the words "girl," "boy," "lamp" and "sweater," but we do not have simple words for half a lamp or part of a sweater. We must detect the critical features of an event and exaggerate them if we are to use language categories efficiently. If hair length and bone structure were given equal weight no decision could be made about the sex of the person.

Similarly, if a child feels he is just a little better in art than his peers, he is tempted to exaggerate that difference and believe he is *much* better, or even the best, in art. This process helps to build a generalized expectancy of success. The teacher must recognize and praise as many areas of competence as possible, approaching as an unattainable goal the number of unique talents in the classroom. A prize for every skill is the ideal to be realized. Competence is, after all, relative. We must permit each child to hold his own standards for a dimension of mastery in which he has special talent.

The waning of motivation in school during the middle elementary years, in contrast to the enthusiasm of the primary grades, occurs in part because the ten-year-old has established his role in the classroom. He is, for the moment, relatively certain about where he stands in relation to his peers and teachers, and his motivation for gaining more information about himself is less urgent than it had been in earlier years. The school can rekindle this motive by changing classroom conditions so that the child is no longer completely certain of his place, so that it is a little more difficult for him to predict what is going to happen each day or how he will fare in an exercise or a contest. Mild uncertainty vitalizes the latent need to know the self better. Some teachers utilize this principle when they grade bright children a little lower than they deserve, to prevent what they regard as overconfidence and subsequent apathy. But the same principle holds for the less competent pupil. When a child is certain he will fail, he also becomes apathetic. All children should be unsure—but only just a little unsure—of their performance in the classroom.

Psychological uncertainty is one of man's major motivating forces. It intrudes into the stream of mental life whenever a deviation from the established norm is encountered. Sometimes the uncertainty is imposed by others rather than self-generated and the person tries to deal with the intruder; if he cannot, distress grows. Efforts to gain friendship, praise, recognition, or power often arise from the urgent need to keep uncertainty within reasonable bounds. On other occasions the person generates the uncertainty by recognizing a discrepancy between some idealized performance and his own capacities. If he possesses a strategy to close the gap, he will activate a motive for mastery, and the accompanying emotion will be excitement, interest, or even wonder, rather than fear, anxiety, or shame. The motive for mastery can be gratified in almost any context, from backyard to bedroom, and lies at the heart of man's love of challenge. But when the goal is attained, boredom—or even apathy—replaces zeal and a new prize is sought. The child as well as the adult likes to test himself, and a healthy society provides him with a variety of arenas in which such self-examination can thrive.

ANGER AND THE MOTIVE OF HOSTILITY

The emotion of anger arises from conditions that are almost the reverse of those that produce uncertainty, for anger is provoked when one is certain that a person or object is imposing—or may impose—a threat or frustration. There is a parallel between the subtle emotional feeling of uncertainty and the subsequent motive to resolve it and the emotion of anger and the subsequent motive of hostility. Two types of experiences are likely to provoke anger, and once this emotion is aroused the person will want to remove, hurt, or injure the individual or object that he believes caused his anger. This motive is called *hostility*.

Sources of Anger. A major source of anger is the interruption of a response routine. Any interruption—actual or potential—of a sequence of behavior directed at a goal can provoke anger. For example, a child is watching television and his brother changes the channel, or the older brother simply warns the child that he is going to take the television away in twenty minutes. The internal sensations created by such an interruption are one component of anger. A second component is the child's perception of the cause of the interruption. If he thinks he knows the source of the frustration, anger develops and is likely to be accompanied by a hostile wish to hurt, physically or psychologically, the cause of the interruption. Let us note again the parallel with uncertainty. Just as a discrepant event that cannot be handled provokes the alerted state of uncertainty, so the blocking of a goal-directed action provokes anger. Uncertainty leads to a motive to resolve it; anger leads to the motive of hostility.

A second source of anger is a threat or challenge to a person's standards—to what he believes to be both true and good. Name-calling is a classic illustration. A ten-year-old becomes angry if he is called stupid, ugly, or afraid because he has been prevented from carrying out a potential response routine. A person's actions flow from his beliefs, and a threat to the validity of these beliefs leaves his behavior without rational foundation. A child would not study if he believed he were unintelligent and could not master a subject. An adolescent boy would not try to establish a relationship with a girl if he were sure he was unattractive. The undermining of standards is always a potential block to future action.

Most of the occasions for anger and hostility arise when we are prevented from behaving in a way that matches our desires or our preferred beliefs about ourselves. This mismatch breeds resentment, for we want our behavior and beliefs to be in harmonious accord. As the child matures his anger becomes increasingly directed at people who are potential threats to the attainment of a goal or to standards that he would like to maintain. It is generally the case that we become angry only at people who threaten us—either by frustrating our desires or by preventing us from holding standards that we find pleasing. Most people are indifferent to the vast majority of others they meet; they are angry or hostile toward a very small proportion of the people they know.

An adolescent boy feels intense hatred for the young man who he suspects may steal his girlfriend. A young college woman resents her mother's excessive concern with clothes and appearance because she wants to believe her family cares about socially important issues. The mother's behavior threatens the daughter's standards. Whenever someone is a potential threat to the attainment of a desired goal or to the maintenance of a standard, anger and hostility are likely to develop. Since beauty, love, power, wealth, and status are among the prized goals in our society, the people who control access to these prizes are usually targets of hostility.

The simmering of anger between husbands and wives is usually due to the inability of each partner to gratify the motives of the other. The wife may want continuing reassurance that she is loved and is vital to the functioning of the family. If her husband does not allow her to hold this standard, she grows resentful. The husband may need to believe he is the final arbiter of decisions or the stabilizing figure in the home. If his wife does not support this belief, he too grows angry. Our culture's emphasis on the significance of sexual pleasure may lead each partner to feel the other is inadequate and to blame the other for a frustration that is, in all likelihood, of mutual origin.

Anger Versus Anxiety. An unpleasant feeling tone following a discrepant event is common to both anxiety and anger. If the source of the feeling cannot be specified, or there is uncertainty over its termination, anxiety is generated. If the source can be specified and the outcome is predictable, anger is the dominant reaction. For example, if a person is not sure why he failed a task, he becomes anxious. If someone suggests that he is basically incompetent, he becomes angry. Anger occurs when a person mobilizes his attention on a relatively specific cause of discomfort, or more accurately, on what he believes to be the cause of the discomfort.

Anger does not always occur whenever a child's actions are

interrupted. If he does not know what interrupted his behavior—what caused the tower to fall—he may become afraid rather than angry. If someone takes a toy from him, he begins to rage and protest. However, if someone were to gradually lift the toy away from him, as if by an invisible force, the child will become alerted and uncertain and will probably display fear rather than anger. Consider a man's experience with a door that will not open. The man will feel anger at another person if he believes that someone locked the door from the other side. He will become angry with himself if he believes that the door is stuck because he failed to oil the lock before the winter began. But if the man is sure that the door is neither locked nor stuck, and unsure as to why it will not open, uncertainty and anxiety will occur. The door becomes a discrepant event that he cannot explain.

Whether anxiety or anger arises in a particular situation depends on the person's interpretation of the experience. Anxiety occurs when he has no immediate explanation for a discrepant event that blocks a response routine. Anger occurs when he believes that he knows the cause of the thwarting of his actions. Several intriguing implications follow from this analysis. People who do not reflect upon possible explanations of frustrating events are apt to become angry; people who pause to analyze the situation are likely to become anxious. The national unrest in America prior to the 1968 presidential election made many intellectuals anxious because they realized that no one person or group was to blame for the strife that was tearing at the nation's spirit. "The conditions and the times" were held responsible, but people cannot become angry with an entity as abstract as "the conditions and the times." Other segments of the population became angry at the hippies, the blacks, college students, or all three groups, because they believed these people were the cause of social unrest. Many citizens voted for George Wallace out of anger and hostility to those who wanted Humphrey or McCarthy elected. They wanted to hurt those citizens who had frustrated them. The more knowledge a person has about a frustrating situation that has no clear or simple cause, the less likely he will be to respond with anger. But the more knowledge he has about a situation that does have a clear cause, the more likely he is to become angry, especially if the cause is human.

The child passes through developmental stages during which the balance of anger and anxiety changes. During the first three years, when the child has few explanations for unusual actions, he is likely to become frightened, not angry, at human behavior that he finds strange or unfamiliar. As he approaches school age and develops some fixed ideas as to causes, the balance shifts toward anger as a more common reaction to the uncomfortable feelings generated by discrepant actions in others. The eight-year-old cruelly teases a child who limps, throws stones at a bus carrying black children to his school, or rages at his failure to be included in a play group. The three-year-old, in contrast, does not become angry in any of these situations. The older child is more prone to anger because he places the source of his uncertainty and discomfort in the external world. A child's mood will quickly change from fear to anger if he realizes, or persuades himself, that the sudden turning off of the light in his room, which he cannot understand, is a trick perpetrated by someone. When the initially frightened child realizes that the source of his discomfort is human, he complains angrily, "Why did you scare me?"

The child is often uncomfortable and anxious in school because he cannot do the assigned work. However, it is easy for him to decide that parents or teachers are the source of his discomfort. Any anxiety he may have felt initially will be dispelled and replaced by resentment toward them, for if they had not forced him to go to school and to work at problems he could not solve, he would not feel so uncomfortable. The child may blame his parents and teachers for his "being in school" and have an unconscious desire to hurt them for this frustration. This wish can find expression in inattention in school or unruliness at home. The most serious threat to the child is the possibility of failure. Some children will be unable to blame either the teacher or the parent for the frustration of failure, and they will become anxious. Similarly, if the child cannot gain acceptance by his peer group and cannot blame anyone for this failure, he will become anxious. If the source of his rejection is specifiable, he may become angry and devise ways to injure or annoy his persecutor.

The teacher is also prone to anger. A noisy child interrupts her lesson; a bright child cannot learn the lesson she prepared. The teacher's anger often leads to hostility because she believes that she knows the source of her irritation. And she acts to eliminate it.

She sends the noisy boy to the office; she tells the bright child he is not paying attention; she keeps the class after school. She scolds and scolds and scolds. She blames the size of the class, the absence of curriculum materials, the long hours—everything and everyone but herself. If the teacher understood more clearly the complexity of the classroom environment and made a more careful diagnosis of the cause of her irritations, she might be more constructive.

The anger of many college students arises from their beliefs about the causes of their frustration and distress. The average nineteen-year-old is unsure of his future and of the values he should adopt. He is plagued by uncertainty and vague feelings of isolation. Like the young child, he is confronted with many specifiable sources of frustration—examinations, term papers, indifferent professors, large classes, the war in Vietnam, and social injustice. Since each of these phenomena also elicits discomfort, he unconsciously places the full blame for his dyspeptic mood on these immediately accessible targets. He is angry and wants to hurt those who he believes are the sources of his anguish. He openly criticizes his courses, his professors, his university, and the institutions of society. On occasion he attacks their property. Although his anger at these targets is not without some justification, it is amplified by the additional anguish generated by the personal uncertainties of his daily life.

As indicated earlier, the wish to hurt the irritating object is the most likely consequence of anger. It is relatively easy for hostility to follow anger because of the close relation in time and space between the uncomfortable feeling of anger and the object or person causing it. The source of anger is usually present and specifiable. Since human beings continually frustrate or threaten others, by intention or accident, it is inevitable that hostility will develop. As people crowd together in smaller and smaller living areas, it becomes increasingly easy to blame others for personal distress, and anger and hostility may come to displace anxiety as a prepotent reaction to the daily discomforts of everyday living.

Secondary Motives. Like uncertainty, hostility also leads to a variety of secondary motives, including mastery, power, recognition, affection, and dominance. There are many ways to hurt another person. Direct physical attack is the most obvious, but teasing, criticism, and threat are also effective. Less frequently the achievement of mastery and recognition, the acquisition of power and wealth, and sexual behavior can gratify a hostile wish. Let us consider how each of these apparently nonaggressive behaviors might gratify hostility.

A ten-year-old boy resents a less intelligent classmate who bullies him continually. The boy might strive for good grades in school in order to threaten the bully by making him feel he is less intelligent than his victim. The acquisition of power can be used to humble another who covets status. A person "gets even" with another by gaining more of what the enemy values, be it strength, power, money, or honorary degrees. Sexual behavior can also gratify hostility. A woman with an inattentive husband initiates an affair out of anger; a man who hates women uses sexual behavior to defile them. This writer recalls talking with a nineteen-year-old college woman who was engaging in promiscuous sexual behavior with older male friends of her father in the hope that he would discover her actions. She wanted to "shake him up" for his past indifference toward her.

Thus the same motives and goal-related actions that resolve uncertainty can also serve to gratify hostility. The child can work hard in school to reduce anxiety over parental displeasure or to displace a younger brother and cause him grief. An adolescent can obtain a power position with his peers in order to be free of the uncertainty he feels when others dominate him or to frustrate a rival who wishes to control the group. An adolescent girl may do poorly in school because she wants to avoid the responsibility and uncertainty of being placed in a situation in which consistently high performance will be expected of her or because she wants to disappoint her aloof, demanding mother. The public goal sought by the child is rarely a faithful clue to his basic intentions. This is one reason why some books of parental advice are of questionable value.

How shall we regard the goal-directed behaviors that seem to be aimed at gaining mastery, power, dominance, affection, sexual pleasure, or recognition? For example, should an action that hurts another person be called aggressive even though the intention is not to injure anyone? Should any action that serves hostility be called aggressive, even though it does not hurt anyone? We probably should not use the word "aggressive" to describe behavior, for it implies a hostile intention that may not be present. The same suggestion is relevant for dependent behavior. All dependent acts are not the product of anxiety. Behavior is most profitably described—or categorized—by diagnosing its intention and noting its context, rather than by examining its final effect in the world. We call all acts of adolescent crime aggressive because they seem to have the common effect of injuring property or people. But these behaviors can stem from many different motives and can occur under different circumstances. We regard drug-taking as indicative of a motive for escape and ignore the many other possible reasons for the action and the situation in which the action occurs. Taking heroin in a party setting in order to avoid teasing by friends is different in an important way from shooting heroin alone in order to escape depression. We must always ask about the primary intentions of the action and the situations that provoked the motive and maintained the behavior.

It may seem odd that sexual motivation is the last rather than the first motive to be discussed, considering Freud's emphasis on sexuality. Sexual motivation is important in childhood, but is probably not as relevant as control of uncertainty, mastery, and hostility to the work of the school. The most important distinction between sexuality and the other three motives is that the former is primarily a sensory motive, whereas the latter are not.

There is a small set of sensations that people report as pleasant, and the source of the pleasure can be traced to the discharge of specific receptor areas on or within the body. A sweet taste, cessation of pain, warmth, genital stimulation, and orgasm are among this group. The mental representations of these sensory states are called *sensory motives*. Although it is obvious that people wish to repeat events that are physically pleasant (one four-year-old boy refers to his penis as "happiness"), the conditions that determine pleasantness are not always clear. Sensory motives rarely exist in pure form and are usually associated with the other motives just considered.

The primary goal of sexual motivation is the sensory pleasure derived from genital stimulation. The primary goal for the other three motives is not a sensory experience but a cognitive state. Of course, cognitive representations of symbolic goals do become associated with the sensory pleasure of sexuality. A man may experience sexual excitement when he sees a female undressed, when he hears a sexy joke, or when a perfumed woman brushes up against him. An infinite number of events and ideas can become linked with sexual excitement and each can serve as a goal for the primary sexual motive. Moreover, the primary motive is not synonymous with the desire to be masculine or feminine or the motives for dating, marriage, love, and promiscuity. Each of these secondary motives and relevant actions can serve the primary sexual motive but can also gratify the motives discussed earlier.

Sexual Behavior in Preadolescence. Although the primary sexual motive for sensory pleasure probably does not undergo much change with development, the secondary motives associated with it do. During the first few years of life the sensory motive is dominant. In the preschool and early school years, however, many children develop affectionate relations with the parent of the opposite sex, and secondary motives to see the parent nude or to obtain physical affection become ascendant.

These sexual motives are important aspects of the affectionate bond between the child and the parent of the opposite sex, and they make the child more receptive to adopting the values of that parent. However, the anxiety generated by sexual feelings toward the parent can create conflict and symptoms like phobias and nightmares. Sexual wishes and masturbatory behavior can conflict with a standard (inconsistency between two beliefs or between a belief and a behavior) and may generate anxiety and the subsequent desire to alleviate the distress. The child expects punishment for these motives, and his preferred reaction is to behave in a way that will make parental punishment unlikely. The strategy is to become obedient to parental requests, do well in school, or become responsible, honest, trustworthy, or virtuous—depending on what values the parents promote. There is only one danger in this dynamic. If the anxiety over sexual motivation is unusually intense and the accompanying guilt pervasive, the child may deprecate himself and come to the conclusion that he cannot do anything well. Excessive guilt over sexual motives can provoke the child to seek punishment. The child may misbehave in unusual and inexplicable ways. He may become irritatingly mischievous or annoying, and his behavior may be puzzling to his parents. These reactions can be the child's way of inviting punishment as an atonement for his violations of prohibited thoughts and actions.

Sexual Behavior in Adolescence. During the early adolescent years the dominant secondary motive is the desire to establish heterosexual relationships. The adolescent combines the strong desire for sexual gratification with wishes for psychological intimacy with others and for relationships that will enhance his self-concept.

There is much concern over the permissive attitude toward sexual behavior held by contemporary adolescents. But even if we could produce statistics that reflect the relative frequency of sexual acts for young adults in 1970, 1950, 1930, and 1910, the number of episodes of intercourse would not give us insight into the essential issue. The attitude toward the act and its functional role in human interaction are the important themes. The parents and grandparents of today's young adults usually sanctify sexual behavior in marriage and vilify it before marriage. This arbitrary blend of values distorts sexuality and removes it from the realm of everyday human activity. Contemporary young adults have repaired this astigmatism. They have stripped sexual behavior of both the sacredness and the shame that is characteristic of the attitude of older generations.

There is much health in this attitude. The price to be paid, if any, concerns the depth of the relation between the partners. Bonds between adults are often self-serving and fragile, kept taut by illusion. Sexuality has been an important component of that illusion. The sanctification of sexual behavior, though perhaps unnatural, constrains action and retards the inevitable wearing away of the sexual mystique. If the discoveries of sexual joy are made many years before a marriage partner is selected, it is less likely that intense passion will, like ambrosia, persuade the partners that they are privileged to a precious rite.

The Relationship
Between Motives and Behavior

DEVELOPMENTAL CHANGES IN MOTIVES

Since the desire to keep uncertainty within a narrow band is a pervasive human trait, the dominant motives during any period of life are often centered on those goals whose gratification is a little uncertain. Hence we can better understand the changing motives of the growing child by examining the major sources of uncertainty. If a person is certain that a goal can or cannot be had with ease, there will be no activation of the motive for that goal. The motives that are preoccupying are usually those linked to goals that one is uncertain of attaining. These foci of doubt change as the child matures.

Infancy and Early Childhood. During the first four months of life the infant has few, if any, mental representations of future goals and therefore no motives. The causes of his actions reside in other forces. A newly hatched turtle crawls over yards of wet sand toward the sea with no image of the sea and no idea of where it is going. The conditions of light and shadow created by the moonlight on the water elicit the directional locomotion. So too with the very young infant. Some objects or situations invite responses because they are attractive in appearance or produce pleasant, exciting stimulation. The movement of a mobile is sufficient incentive to elicit hitting it. It does not help us to understand the child's response if we say that he *wanted* to hit it. Many events can elicit specific actions from the infant, but these actions are not necessarily guided by an idea of a desired goal.

As the child approaches the second half of the first year his first motives emerge. An example of this new maturity is seen in the nine-month-old child who reaches for a toy he saw hidden under a pillow, as if he knew it was there. When he shows surprise that it is gone, he is telling us that he expected to find the toy, that he had a mental representation of the object. We therefore infer that he was motivated. The young child in a typical family is certain of food and warm clothing and unaware of the problem of peer acceptance; thus he is not preoccupied with attaining these goals. He is uncertain, however, about the presence of his parents and their affection. Desire for these goals becomes dominant during the second year. When a child is in a strange house and cannot see or touch his mother, he becomes distressed if she does not return. His need for her presence dominates his consciousness, and no other prize, no matter how attractive, can lead him to forget his fear.

As the child enters his third year he learns to reassure himself that his mother's absence is temporary, and this source of uncertainty diminishes. But now a related motive becomes dominant. The child becomes uncertain about his mother's attitude toward him, her signs of approval, disapproval, punishment, and rejection. He becomes sensitive to any information about her feelings for him. The desire for some sign of positive evaluation dominates his earlier wish for her presence. This motive remains dominant until the fourth year of life, when a new source of uncertainty emerges. The four-year-old becomes concerned with his power and autonomy in relation to parents and siblings. His mother orders him to go to bed, to eat, to wash, to stop making noise, to stop teasing his sister, to stop picking at his meat. The constraints on his actions are frustrating and he cannot predict when they will occur. His uncertainty over these events pushes the motives for autonomy and dominance to the top of the hierarchy. The child becomes preoccupied with whether he will be able to resist intrusions into his activity, whether he will be coerced into submission, whether he will be able to control others. He is still motivated for affection and positive evaluation but is now a little more certain of these prizes. Hence, when the issue of autonomy and dominance arises, the motive for affection takes a subordinate position.

The struggle to preserve one's autonomy of action and choice is threatened most seriously during the preschool years, and the need to control this potential threat becomes of paramount concern to the child. The desire to dominate others is based on the need to reduce uncertainty over future interactions with other people. The child rebels at the tension of not knowing whether the next person he will meet will force him into submission, will intrude upon his actions, or more seriously, will attack him in some way. When he is assured of a dominant position in the interaction, his uncertainty is quieted.

The Early School Years. As the child approaches school age he begins to base his conception of himself on his competence at culturally valued skills. The one-year-old who learns to walk, talk, and run is perfecting a set of coordinations that are natural to all children and hence easy to attain. School-related skills, however, are less natural—millions of children all over the world never learn to read, write, or add—and more difficult to attain. Children evaluate their competence at these skills in part by comparing themselves with

65

others. Unfortunately, the child assumes that if he is less talented than another, he is also less worthy. The child is not sure he can read, spell, or play baseball, and he wants to know once and for all whether he is able to gain expertise at these skills. He is also uncertain about his ability to form friendships. Hence competence and peer acceptance become major sources of uncertainty during the early school years, and the motives to attain these goals are ascendant in the motive hierarchy.

Adolescence. During early adolescence sexual motives make an initial claim for salience. Western culture has persuaded every fourteen-year-old that sexual attractiveness is important, and the young adolescent is unsure of this new challenge. The first dates of the adolescent are exquisite illustrations of the attempt to determine sexual effectiveness, poise, and responsiveness. A new source of uncertainty breaks the surface of awareness, and the motives for praise, dominance, mastery, and acceptance move over and give this new wish a more central place in the psychic space.

The young adolescent also feels uncertain about the integrity of his beliefs and about whether he holds a coherent set of moral principles that can guide action. He worries about the fact that he believes in God but some of his friends do not, and he broods about which conclusion is correct. He wants to base his moral decisions on his own values, rather than on the opinions of his parents, but he is not sure what his moral principles are. In short, the adolescent experiences uncertainty over his ideology. Campus unrest, the damning of adult authority, and occasionally apathy are the consequences of this moral void. These disquieting phenomena will continue until young adults find a code of values to which they are willing to give spiritual commitment.

It is helpful to conceptualize stages in human development in terms of changing foci of uncertainty. The major uncertainties, like irritants, force the system to deal with them and, in the process of coping, produce change. As the child matures his goals become more symbolic and less dependent on overt action. The three-year-old wants to be hugged; the eight-year-old wants some sign or indication that he is valued. The four-year-old wants to see his brother cry; the fourteen-year-old merely wants to know that his brother is upset.

When an adult has gratified a motive it is usually the case that he has finally experienced the thought he wanted—or the thought that he thought he wanted.

As noted earlier, there is neither a simple nor a necessary relation between a motive and an action aimed at gratifying it. First, a motive need not lead to any behavior. A boy can be motivated to date a girl but may make no attempt to gratify the wish. Second, an action can serve any one of several motives. The primary motive behind a particular response is rarely obvious. One boy may set fire to a school in order to experience sexual excitement and orgasm; another to express hostility to a teacher; a third to be caught and to obtain notoriety among his friends. The external act of arson is the same, but the motives are dramatically different.

There are five major factors that determine whether or not a motive will be expressed in action. These factors are (1) the likelihood that a situation will activate the motive; (2) the degree to which strong feelings accompany the motive; (3) the availability of actions that can gratify the motive; (4) freedom from the anxiety and conflict that inhibit action; and (5) the person's confidence that the action will lead to a desired goal.

Activation of the Motive. Motives, like all ideas, exist in either latent or active form. Every person has hundreds of thousands of ideas that lie dormant until he happens to encounter a scene that evokes them. A man may know that Nepal is in northern India but may never call upon that fact until someone asks him or he reads a headline about fighting on the Indian border. Even the most hostile child does not walk around all day hating people. The motive is activated only when he is thwarted or threatened, and hostile action is most likely to occur following activation of the motive.

As the child matures the activation of motives become less dependent on external circumstances and more closely related to his thoughts. The four-year-old sees someone with an ice cream cone and wants one; he sees his mother caring for his infant sister and suddenly craves attention. The adult's motives are more independent of immediate events in the environment. A young man who has been wronged by a friend may be driven for years by a desire for revenge, without benefit of seeing the target of his hate. Of course, not all the adult's motives are completely independent of the external environment. A pretty girl, a traffic jam, or a challenging golf course can jar a motive from latent to active form.

The teacher can activate the child's motive for mastery by linking it to existing motives that are ascendant for him. For example, the average first grader wants the teacher's praise and acceptance. He believes that a positive response from this "good" person implies that he is also "good." The child wants the teacher to approve of his performance and, by implication, of him. He wishes to avoid her disapproval, for it implies that he is bad. If adults are viewed as good, or at least as more good than bad, the profile of actions and objects that adults praise will help the child to decide which things in the world, including himself, are good. This "laying on" of value works like King Midas' golden touch.

One of the serious liabilities of building larger and larger school units in the service of economy and efficiency is that it increases the depersonalization within the school. A ten-year-old is lost in the midst of one hundred and fifty other ten-year-olds whose art teacher attends all five fifth grades. College undergraduates are protesting against this terrible sacrifice to size, and many colleges must begin to create new structures. Elementary schools and high schools should begin to break up larger units into smaller ones. If a new elementary school for a thousand pupils is being planned, it should not be given one name and viewed as one institution. Rather, it should be given six names and regarded as six separate schools that happen to be on the same property. Thus a first-grade child will be in the only "grade" in his school, and upon graduation there will be six valedictorians rather than one, six prize-winning poems rather than one, and six times as many opportunities for students to participate in the creative and constructive activities of the school. Such a procedure would enable more children to believe in their individual worth. The more the child actively shares in the prizes that the community values, the more salient his motive for mastery and the healthier the school atmosphere.

Accompaniment of Strong Feelings. Motives are often accompanied by strongly felt sensations from the heart, stomach, muscles, and skin. These feelings form the basis of the emotions we call anger, loneliness, sadness, passion, and excitement. We are more aware of our motives when they are accompanied by strong feelings, for the distinctive experience of joy, pain, anger, or sexual excitement cannot be ignored. These emotions activate motives—thoughts appropriate to certain goals—and maintain our attention on them. As a result, action is likely to occur. When our motives are not accompanied by strong feelings, we tend to forget about related goals and concentrate on other domains of interest.

A person is not always aware of the motives to which his emotions properly belong, and a strong emotion can provoke a variety of behaviors. A four-year-old child may be irritable because he is hungry but may not be aware of the source of his irritation. If the feeling occurs during a quarrel with an older brother, it is likely to increase the child's hostility toward him. Every mother has an awareness of this phenomenon, for she excuses aggressive or mischievous behavior at 11:30 that she would not excuse earlier in the morning by noting, "It is close to Johnny's lunchtime and he always gets nasty then."

The number of basic emotional states is a continuing puzzle to psychologists. Some people argue that there are as many emotions as there are words for different kinds of feelings. Thus "sad," "depressed," "mournful," "grief-stricken," and "apathetic" refer to different emotions, for we have a different association to each of these words. Psychologists are generally disquieted by this casual attitude toward emotion, however, for it allows us to make up new emotional states each day merely by finding new names to describe how we feel. An alternative and more reasonable view is that there is a small set of emotional states that can be differentiated, and that all other emotions are derivatives of this basic set. If this assumption is true, how can we determine the basic set? Observations of infants, complemented by studies of chimpanzees, suggest at least six basic emotional states: distress, fear, anger, depression, excitement, and contentment. These six emotions may be primary because of their distinctive feeling tone and characteristic association with certain bodily postures, facial expressions, and vocal sounds.

Distress and fear. Both infants and young chimpanzees whine and whimper when they are removed from their mother, are in pain, or are in a situation that is physically uncomfortable. This distress state occurs in all mammals. Fear is aroused by situations that are discrepant or that directly threaten the physical integrity of the animal. These conditions elicit tendencies to withdraw and characteristic facial expressions. The chimpanzee shows retraction of the ears and lips; the child shows widening of the eyes and retraction of the skin on the forehead. Spontaneous defecation and urination often occur when animal or child is intensely fearful.

Anger. As we have seen, anger is generated when a goal-directed action is either interrupted or threatened. Such a situation usually leads to increased motor action, lowering of the eyes, staring, and often a vocal outburst. The rage displayed by a chimpanzee who has been chased from an eating area resembles the kicking and thrashing of a three-year-old who has been carried forcefully from the backyard into the house. Chimpanzees also seem to show reactions that resemble human jealousy. Jane Goodall reports that a female chimpanzee being attended by half a dozen males bristled with anger when a younger female came into the area. The males quickly turned their attention to the younger animal. Following the unexpected rejection, the older female's hair stood erect—a reaction typically seen in anger—and she sauntered over to the younger female and began poking at her.

Depression. The emotion of depression, or apathy, is occasioned by loss of an object of attachment. Both chimpanzee and child show lassitude, loss of appetite, and sluggishness when they lose their parent—a combination of traits that we associate with depression. This syndrome occurs when the child knows the goal he wants but is unable to attain it, when he is helpless to obtain a desired goal. Depression thus contrasts nicely with anger, which is an active response to the thwarting of a desired goal. The shift from anger to sadness is often seen when two people sever a love relation. Initially, one partner is angry at the rejection and may even make an attempt to restore the tie. If he is unsuccessful, and still in love, he is likely to become depressed, if only temporarily.

Excitement and contentment. Excitement is a pleasant emotion that most often occurs when the child encounters a discrepant event that he can assimilate because he has an appropriate response to make. A ten-month-old child watches a small car roll down a wooden incline, hit a doll at the bottom, and knock it down. During the first five or six occurrences of this event the child looks puzzled;

he is quiet, subdued, and attentive. By the ninth occurrence he smiles as the car rolls down the incline, on the tenth he laughs, and on the eleventh he is laughing, babbling, and highly excited. The child finally understands the event and can integrate it into his experience. This simple example captures the essence of excitement. The child feels eager anticipation on the first day of school or before a carnival, a date, or a plane trip. In each case, an unusual event has occurred or is about to occur, and the child is prepared to deal with it. Fear and excitement are both preceded by the unusual. But fear arises when there is no available way of coping with the event; excitement occurs when the person is prepared. Contentment can be seen in the purring of a cat, the murmuring of a chimpanzee when he is being groomed, the smile of pleasure in a baby when he is being stroked or fed, and the relaxed mood following orgasm. The major difference between contentment and excitement is the level of arousal.

Possession of Appropriate Responses. The possession of responses that can gratify a motive also controls the child's behavior. It should be obvious that a one-year-old cannot effectively hurt his older brother or play baseball, even if he were motivated to do so. He does not possess the actions that might gratify the wish. Many behaviors are learned by watching others and by inferring the relation between motive and action. Thus the five-year-old learns that teasing can hurt; that yelling is an effective way to threaten others; that confession is a means of avoiding punishment.

Freedom from Anxiety and Conflict. Anxiety is a continual threat to the expression of goal-directed behavior. The changing mores on sexual behavior are a good example of this principle. In earlier generations adolescent girls were aroused sexually and possessed relevant behaviors, but sexual expression violated their standards and elicited anxiety, and they were led to inhibit sexual action. Contemporary adolescent girls engage more frequently in sexual behavior primarily because they feel less anxiety over its expression, not because the motive has become more salient or passion stronger.

Anxiety over motivated actions that violate standards builds through the first decade of life and then stabilizes. Hence during the period from three to ten years of age there is apt to be an increasingly disguised relation between a child's motives and his behavior. During adolescence anxiety over gratifying certain motives attenuates as the adolescent persuades himself that it is childish to be afraid of expressing resentment toward a parent or sexual wishes toward a love object. The relation between the adolescent's motives and his actions becomes more direct.

As noted earlier, inconsistency between two ideas is an important source of uncertainty and anxiety. When the inconsistent ideas are motives, the person is said to be in *conflict*. Many conflicts that derive from contradictory wishes can influence behavior in the classroom. For example, the desire for a teacher's approval is opposed by a motive "to be mature," which is characterized by independence from adults and a coolness to their praise. A young girl's wish to perform well in mathematics is opposed by her desire to maintain sex-role standards, which emphasize unusual competence at mathematics as a masculine trait. The wish to get better grades in order to gain recognition contradicts a motive to be cooperative rather than excessively competitive with others. Or the wish to excel may be opposed by the fear that one will not be able to perform continually at a high level. In sum, the motives for praise, recognition, mastery, and power, which push the child to work in school, often conflict with motives with an opposite set of goals. This conflict produces uncertainty, anxiety, and eventually inhibition.

Sex-role conflict. During the primary grades a young boy's reluctance to violate sex-role standards can interfere with his involvement in school. Most children view the school as a feminine place because women run the classroom. This perception violates the boy's desire to make his talents and behavior congruent with a masculine standard, and his zeal for school mastery is diluted. The college student's involvement in school is also affected by the desire to maintain sex-role standards. Masculine standards place preferential value on pragmatic knowledge and on special competence in mechanics, mathematics, science, and business. Academic subjects that have little instrumental effect on the world or that are primarily verbal—such as English, history, and foreign languages—are viewed as feminine. Thus it is not uncommon for a young man to be doing well in physics but failing history or English, while his female counterpart is doing fine in English but is unable to pass her physical science requirement.

It is an unfortunate fact that the legitimacy of domains of knowledge is influenced by sex-role standards, and the teacher should be aware of potential conflicts. One useful suggestion is to masculinize the primary-grade classroom so that more boys can be persuaded that school is "man's" work as much as "woman's." The optimal strategy is to place male as well as female teachers in the classroom. Since this is difficult to do at the present time, the teacher might segregate her students for some part of the day so that reading and number lessons are held in all-boy or all-girl settings. The teacher can then introduce materials that are maximally interesting to boys or to girls, rather than using texts and problems that attempt to appeal to both sexes and are often insipid.

It is possible that the changing sex-role values of our culture will minimize this conflict in the years ahead and make these suggestions obsolete. But at the moment a large proportion of boys in the first few grades, especially those whose fathers are not in academic or professional vocations, view the school enterprise as feminine. We should try to remedy this maladaptive perception.

Conflict over autonomy. The young boy's desire to develop a sense of autonomy as well as a masculine sex-role identity often leads him to resist complete obedience to the teacher, for he views the act of passive submission as both childish and feminine. He is pushed to defy the teacher occasionally and to resist conforming to her requests.

The desire for autonomy also creates conflicts for the college student. For example, a young woman who has worked diligently since school entrance and has an excellent record suddenly decides two months before graduation that she is going to withdraw from college to write a novel, join the Peace Corps, or work for civil rights—each a commendable and socially relevant action. But a few hours of friendly talk reveal the root cause of this decision. The young woman believes that her diligence was motivated in part by a desire to please her parents. She feels she has worked for them, and that graduation is their victory, not hers. Thus to graduate is to admit that she allowed fear of her parents' displeasure to motivate her, and she feels childish. The young woman holds a standard for maturity and autonomy that dictates, "There should be no fear of adult disapproval; one must work for personal goals." She cannot decide if she wants to graduate because she wants the degree or because she desires her parents' approval. The doubt grows and cannot be resolved, and the decision to withdraw is an escape from the uncertainty.

Some of the defiance of the college student also arises from doubts over autonomy. The student suspects his motives: Is he studying biology because he wants to be a doctor or because he wants to obtain the approval of his parents and teachers? It is much like fighting ghosts in a dark room, as if someone heard the command "Breathe" and was not sure if breathing were his idea or another's. It is frightening to work for a goal and to be unsure of why one is seeking it. Escape is one defense.

Since the young child also wants to establish his own values, it is advantageous to persuade the six-year-old of the value and importance of learning intellectual skills. The child is more likely to become motivated to do schoolwork if he believes that the investment of effort is his decision, not the teacher's. For example, the primary-grade teacher might persuade her students of the importance of learning to read by announcing that during one recess period each day no child will be allowed to play with another unless he can first read the child's printed name on the blackboard. The value of clear writing might be promoted by announcing one short period during the day when no child is allowed to speak and any communication to another must be done by written note. These simple procedures can persuade the child of the desirability of academic skills. If the child decides that these skills are valuable—for him—his motivation to master them will be enhanced.

Conflict over power and status. Some children learn to devalue power. Since excellence in school occasionally brings recognition and a position of power and prestige among one's peers, the child may inhibit academic effort in order to avoid assuming a status role with others. There are two major ways in which such a devaluation of power can occur. First, the child may not trust his competence and may fear that if he gains recognition, adults will come to expect outstanding performance from him continually. He is not sure he can deliver excellence all the time and so prefers to remain unnoticed. Second, the child may grow up in a peer or sibling structure in which he is always the scapegoat. As a result, he will develop a negative attitude toward those who rule, who have power over others. The child may decide that the bad rule, the good are ruled. Or he may rationalize his lack of power by deciding that those who have power are corrupt, that no one can attain status, respect, or fame without corrupting his basic values. Thus attainment of power is *de facto* proof of a tainted character. Children and adolescents who have developed a negative view of power may not invest maximal effort in school, for they do not want the recognition and status that unusual talent can bring. Such children must be persuaded that attainment of power can on occasion be beneficial. For most children, of course, the task is just the opposite—they must be persuaded that academic mastery can bring the recognition and status that they value and desire.

Expectancy of Success. Even if a motive is activated, feelings are strong, and the child has a set of effective responses to make, he may not display the responses if he does not believe they will attain the desired goal. For example, most children want to learn to read, but many do not expect to succeed and hence do not involve themselves in the task. A ten-year-old girl who has lived in five foster homes since birth wants affection desperately and knows how to solicit it, but she does not approach others because she is sure her overtures will be rejected.

The belief that an action will gratify a motive determines not only whether the action will be taken but also the ascendancy of the motive in the child's mind. If the child continually expects his desire for friends to be frustrated, the motive will eventually become subordinate to others, and attempts to gain friendship will be rare. As early as three years of age the child learns the pain of failure and wants to avoid it. This aversion stems both from fear of punishment by others and from anxiety over not meeting internalized standards of performance.

The child as well as the adult erects strong defenses against possible failure. For example, a group of four-year-old children was shown a set of ten pictures and asked to recall as many pictures as possible. This is a difficult task for a young child, and most four-year-olds cannot remember more than three pictures. After recalling two pictures, one girl said, "I think I will just tell you one more and then we should do something else." When asked if he could recall any more pictures, a boy replied, "I can't, my mother won't let me, she'd be mad if I said any more."

Compare these statements with those of a twenty-one-year-old college senior who was writing a thesis that would qualify her for graduation with honors. She had written the first chapter, and the instructor, impressed with its quality, praised her excessively and suggested that the final thesis would be outstanding. Four days later the student told the instructor that she would not be able to finish the thesis because she was not feeling well. After twenty minutes of conversation, the young woman admitted that the earlier praise had frightened her; she had become convinced that she would not be able to produce five additional chapters of equal quality and was afraid of disappointing the instructor and herself. Despite the potential delights of graduating with honors, her fear overpowered her desire for success. Man would much rather avoid the pain of failure than taste the sweetness of victory, for when both are possible, he often prefers the former.

IMPLICATIONS FOR THE TEACHER

The power of potential failure to provoke withdrawal is more obvious in children than in adults. The teacher must continually watch for its presence and work at minimizing its insidious effects. She should structure problems and work units so that the child will feel he can master them. Difficult problems should be paced so that potential failure is minimized.

The most serious moment in a classroom is when the child encounters a problem that he does not understand or for which he has no rule to apply. During that short period of time, which feels like an hour, anxiety mounts. If the child is unable to make a response, he will withdraw. It is important that the teacher provide the child with some behavior to initiate for each problem. One good way to achieve this goal is to always give the child two tasks to work on. When one is too difficult he can turn to the other, rather than withdraw from the situation. The teacher often presents problems that leave the child unsure because he does not know how to begin work on them. The Puritan ethic in our society stresses the need to conquer initial frustration in order to build character. If the child perseveres and masters the "hard," he will have learned an important lesson. This is probably true for the child who is fortunate enough to have a hypothesis available to begin work on every problem. But many children are not that gifted or fortunate, and the experience of having no response to make will lead to anxiety. In time, such children withdraw from academic tasks.

The teacher must present problems difficult enough so that they cannot be solved immediately but not so difficult that the child is unlikely to have any hypothesis to initiate during the first minute of study. The best intuitive test of a good curriculum unit is not how many facts it teaches but the degree to which it allows the child to generate new ideas and initiate relevant actions. This is one reason curriculum units for young children that involve concrete materials—such as maps, rulers, paper, glue, stones, and guppies—are often more successful than units that deal with what sounds like an intrinsically interesting idea. For example, many adults are charmed by the provocative question "What will the world be like in the year 2000?" and they assume that the child will be similarly intrigued. However, the young child cannot become involved with this question because he does not have a sufficient reservoir of knowledge to generate many ideas about the year 2000. After a few minutes he becomes bored and restless. The child is not hostile to the problem; he is merely unable to generate a set of relevant ideas. Similarly, high school English teachers often ask the student to write a composition on a theme he knows little about rather than on a topic for which his intuitions and ideas are rich and varied. Before giving an assignment to any child, every teacher should ask herself: "Will the child have an initial set of ideas to begin the task?" If the teacher is not sure of the answer, she should probably restructure the assignment.

An important condition that promotes expectancy of success is the proportion of the child's successes to his failures in the course of the schoolday. Since it is not easy to tailor a curriculum to every child's competence, the school usually selects an average comprehension level that is too easy for the bright child and too difficult for the slow child. The less competent child does not know how to proceed, experiences frequent failure, and becomes apathetic. The teacher should analyze the sequence of work steps in every curriculum unit and should test the size of these steps to determine if the leaps required are too large for some children.

Finally, every child should be given unambiguous feedback on his progress in a task and should be persuaded that his efforts produced the progress. If he feels he is being fed false praise, his expectancy of success will not change to any appreciable degree. The teacher should communicate her confidence in the child's ability to do the task and should give the child praise, when appropriate, as frequently as possible. There is no reason to fear spoiling the child. The young child usually assumes that he cannot do the task anyway, and most, if not all, children are unsure of their ability rather than excessively confident. There is not much danger in overrewarding honest success. Another good strategy is to give special prizes to children who improve in various areas, as well as to students who excel on an absolute level. Finally, the teacher must reduce the child's anxiety over public failure. Some children are terrorized by the possibility of making a mistake in front of the teacher and their classmates. The teacher must create a classroom atmosphere that minimizes this tension and persuades each child that any attempt is more important than avoidance of failure.

Most children in all cultures are driven by the primary motives of control of uncertainty, mastery, hostility, and sexuality. Since this is a rather limited set of motives, we might expect all children to be more similar in psychological structures and behavior than they appear to be. However, there is marked divergence in the secondary motives that flow from these primary forces. The specific goals of the secondary motives are taught by the society and differ across ethnic and cultural groups. The ten-year-old, middle-class child in Evanston, Illinois, is motivated to attain good grades; the ten-year-old child in Guatemala wants to be a better coffee cutter.

The teacher should try to determine the goals each child is seeking and should try to structure classroom activities so that the child will view academic mastery as a means of gratifying the particular motive that is ascendant for him. If the child wants power over peers, the teacher should gratify this desire by placing him in a dominant position in the classroom whenever he shows academic progress. If he wants to be assured of the teacher's acceptance, she should persuade him that this prize will be forthcoming if he makes an effort to read. Every child is motivated for some goal. The teacher must find that goal and graft a motive for academic mastery to it. The teacher must be as good a psychological diagnostician as she is a pedagogue. We must not minimize the difficulty of evaluating the child's tangled nest of wishes. But it is not a hopeless task. Careful analysis of the child can reveal clues. The girl who frequently brings her drawings to the teacher may be seeking recognition; the boy who bullies a peer may be trying to gratify a desire for power. By watching her students carefully and talking with them informally, the teacher can gain more insight into their desires.

The motivation to learn, however, will not lead to much success unless the child has acquired the mental structures and processes necessary for synthesizing information and solving problems. Learning how to extract square roots involves not only sustained attention to the instructions—which is based on motivation—but some knowledge about numbers. Let us now consider the mental structures and processes that complement motivation and enable the child to experience the joy of intellectual growth.

Thought

A nine-year-old listens carefully as the teacher talks about the ancient Egyptian practice of placing dead pharaohs in large pyramids, but he is continually confused because every third sentence contains a word he does not understand. First it is "pyramid," then "mummy," then "Nile," then "desert." He eventually turns his attention to the scene outside the window, for he has lost the thread of the story. The teacher completes the presentation and asks the class to estimate how long it might take to build a pyramid. One child imagines thousands of Egyptian slaves dragging large pieces of stone to the site, intuitively judges that the task would take a long time, and offers the estimate of three years. A second child is completely at sea; no image comes to mind, and with no basis on which to make a guess, he sits quietly. When the teacher asks him directly he murmurs weakly, "I don't know," and upon prodding nervously whispers, "A month?"

Although a child may be highly motivated to learn facts or to solve new problems, motivation is not sufficient. He must also have prior knowledge. The first part of this book was concerned with the motives that promote the acquisition of knowledge and with ways to make the mastery of school skills more attractive to the child. This part examines the mental structures that enable the child to acquire new knowledge and that, in the process, are themselves transformed.

The major difference between a motive and a rule or fact is that the motive is generally accompanied by strong emotional feelings. Since these feelings are stronger than those linked with most knowledge, motives are usually learned more quickly. Moreover, there is no artificial symbolism involved in learning a motive. Affection, praise, coercion, and rejection are readily understood by the young child. But school tasks present him with a puzzling array of letters and numbers. Initially, he does not understand this artificial code and cannot translate it. Imagine a six-year-old suddenly removed from the community he knows and placed among a friendly but strange group of beings who communicated with each other by gesturing with small three-pronged sticks. The child would have difficulty learning expectancies and motives with his new companions. He would be unable initially to interpret their behavior or his effect on them, and he would not know when they were approving or disapproving of him, threatening to hurt him, or offering him friendship. The concepts of arithmetic are not learned as easily as motives because the child does not readily attend to the relevant information, does not have the mental structures necessary to understand the information, and does not work as long at rehearsing the ideas that are central to the concepts.

The first requirement for the learning of any new information, whether it is for solving a problem or for playful enjoyment, is a set of mental structures. These structures give substance to thought and consist of schemata, images, symbols, concepts, and rules. They are the bricks and mortar of the larger structure that is commonly called intelligence.

Mental structures should not be regarded as things, the way we view physical objects; rather, they are potential ways of making sense of experience, of remembering past events, and of solving problems. Gravity is not a thing but a potential force that permits objects to fall to the earth. Similarly, mental structures are abstractions that permit psychological events to be understood and manipulated. These structures are not located in any one place in the mind; nor do they have substance or physical dimension. They are served by a set of cognitive processes, which include perception, memory, evaluation, generation of ideas, and reasoning. The interactions of these mental processes and structures define thought.

There are two distinctly different philosophical attitudes toward human thinking. One view assumes that there is a monitoring function contained within the mental structures and processes themselves that controls mental activity. Thus the thought process can be likened to the reactions in a chemist's beaker. The interaction of the chemical structures of hydrochloric acid and sodium hydroxide produces salt and water; the reaction is inherent in the nature of the chemicals. Some psychologists have been friendly to this view and regard thinking as a more or less mechanical interaction of basic psychological structures. Other psychologists, notably Jean Piaget, assume that higher-order mental structures, more complex than schemata, symbols, concepts, and rules, organize thought and keep it adaptive, coordinated, and efficient. This "executive" psychological function continually monitors mental activity, much as an architect supervises the construction of a house. It decides what the problem is, selects the correct procedures, and knows when the work is done. This second view has a strong appeal. The mind of the ten-year-old is stocked with hundreds of thousands of pieces of information; yet the mind, in its awesome efficiency, quickly selects the correct segment of knowledge and the precise mental routine when asked, "How many feet in four yards?" or "How are a fly and a tree similar?" The following simple demonstration is persuasive of the need to assume a higher-order process that collects and keeps track of what the mind is doing. Ask a child to listen carefully while you say, "8-3-9-1." Pause for a few seconds and then say, "8-9-1." Ask the child which number was omitted the second time. The vast majority of children will answer "3." How can we explain this simple event without assuming that a complex psychological process, something akin to an executive function, is keeping an orderly record of experience and is aware, most of the time, of what the mind knows and where to find it? Let us begin our consideration of thought by turning first to the basic units, the mental structures.

The Structures of Thought

SCHEMATA AND IMAGES

The schema, probably the child's first acquired structure, is a representation of the critical features of a specific event. This representation is neither an image nor a photographic memory of the event. It is perhaps best described as an abstract mental "blueprint," for it preserves the arrangement of a small set of significant elements in the mind. Try to think of your family home as it appeared in childhood. Note that the idea you develop highlights a few critical elements, perhaps an unusual painting, an odd chair, a ladder leaning against the side of the house. The critical elements of the schema give it distinctiveness and differentiate it from similar schemata. For most people, the schema of the Capitol Building in Washington is organized around the dome as the most outstanding feature. The critical element in the Lincoln Memorial is Lincoln's statue; the chair on which he sits and the structure of the larger building are subordinate. The shape of the plot of land on which the monument is located is probably irrelevant. The schema of an object is a little like a cartoonist's caricature of a face, which exaggerates the person's most distinctive features.

An experiment with four-year-olds may provide a clearer understanding of the meaning of a schema. A four-year-old child is given a pile of fifty pictures cut out from magazines, most of which illustrate things that he has no name for and finds strange. He looks at each picture for a few seconds, and when he has finished looking at all fifty he is shown pairs of pictures, each of which contains one picture from the pile he examined earlier and a second picture that he has never seen. He is asked to point to the picture he saw earlier. Most four-year-olds are able to designate forty-five of the fifty pictures correctly. Some get them all right when tested two days later. Adults can look through six hundred pictures and designate over 90 percent correctly. How is this possible?

Let us say that the four-year-old is shown a picture of a slide rule and a picture of a xylophone and correctly points to the slide rule as the picture he saw earlier. We assume that when he first saw the slide rule a schema of its critical elements was registered in his mind. Thus when he looks at the pair of pictures, there is a closer match between the scene of the slide rule and the schema than between the scene of the xylophone and the schema, and "the match" allows him to answer correctly. The potentiality for recognizing the slide rule is inherent in the schema.

An image is a detailed and elaborate mental picture created from a schema. Thus a person's mental image of a friend's face is constructed from his knowledge of the critical features of the face. This "knowledge" is contained in the schema. Perhaps the best way to regard the relationship between a schema and an image is to view the former as the basic skeleton from which a complete and elaborate representation is built when cognitive processes perform work on the schema. One of the major advantages of an image is that it is more easily manipulated in thought.

Symbols are arbitrary names for things and qualities. The best examples of symbols are the names for letters, numbers and objects. If in the previous example the child had said to himself, "That's a ruler," his correct recognition on the test would have been facilitated by the possession of the symbol "ruler." The major difference between a schema and a symbol is that the schema is not arbitrary. It represents a specific sight or sound by preserving the physical relations that were part of the experience. The symbol is an artificial way to code an event, and it is something other than the experience. The child who can name the arbitrary collection of lines we designate as the letter *A,* and can point to an *A* when asked, possesses the symbol for that letter. The child who can remember that he saw the pattern of lines we call *A* but cannot name it or point to it when asked, possesses only the schema for *A.* Of course, children beyond the age of five usually possess both the schema and the symbol for most letters, as well as for many other objects and events. They know that a skull and crossbones symbolizes "danger," that a hexagonal sign at the end of a road symbolizes "stop." Symbols, which do much of the work of the mind, are used to construct the fourth unit of thought—the *concept.*

All concepts are symbols, but they are also much more. They stand for a set of common attributes among a group of schemata, symbols, or images. The critical difference between a symbol and a concept is that the former stands for a specific object or event, whereas the latter represents something common to several objects or events. Consider the drawing of a cross. An eight-month-old child

85

represents this stimulus as a schema. A four-year-old calls it a cross and thus represents it as a symbol. An adult who regards it as the cross of Christianity and imposes on it a relationship to religion and church possesses the concept of "the Cross." When the child learns to read, he initially represents letters as symbols and only later acquires the concepts for letters. He first learns that *D* is the name of a specific line design. He learns later that *D* (or *d's*) have a common attribute—that is, they sound the same and are the first letters of words like "dog" and "door." He has now learned the concept of this letter.

A child's spoken language is not always a good clue as to whether he is using a particular word as a symbol or a concept. If he uses the word "animal" to refer only to his pet dog and never to any other living creature, the word "animal" is functioning for him as a symbol, not as a concept. When he uses this word for a variety of creatures, he has the concept. A two-year-old who says he is "bad" when he soils his pants, but only when he soils his pants, is using the word "bad" as a symbol. When he begins to regard a variety of acts as "bad" he has acquired the concept.

A concept stands for characteristics of events, not for a particular event. A concept represents those attributes that are common to a collection of experiences. The term "religion" usually functions as a concept because there is no single object called religion; rather, there are many events that are characterized by a reference to God and church and a commitment to moral principles. Religion is the concept that summarizes these three dimensions. The concept "dog" refers to the constellation of hair, tail, four feet, elongated face, friendliness to man, and barking sound.

The dimensions of a particular concept can themselves be concepts. "Tail" (which is a dimension of the concept "dog") is itself defined by the dimensions of elongated, thin, flexible, covered with hair, and attached to the rear of a body. There is considerable arbitrariness in whether we call an event a concept or a dimension, especially for abstract concepts. The concept of justice rests on the twin dimensions "evil is defeated" and "good is victorious." But "evil" and "good" are themselves concepts, each defined by its own dimensions.

Concepts can be based on dimensions derived from symbols, images, schemata, or feelings. The concept of the alphabetical letter

O, for example, can rest on the symbol of a circle (○). The young child often calls all round things "balls," where the word "ball" functions for him as a symbol and as a critical dimension for the concept of the letter *O*. The concept of face rests on the schemata for a small set of features common to all faces. The child's concepts of afraid and sick rest on particular feelings. Fear may derive from feelings of sweating, increased heartbeat, and a dry mouth; sickness may be based on a cramp in the stomach and an ache in the head.

A concept is not always associated with a verbal name or language category. A ten-year-old whose father frequently gave him orders may have experienced feelings of resentment toward him. As a result, whenever the boy encounters an older, authoritarian male he feels anger and resentment. The dimensions "old," "male," and "give orders" lead him to experience a particular emotion that, although unnamed, is a *concept*. As the child grows older he may begin to wonder why he has this emotional reaction and may even give it a name. He may say to himself, "Authority bugs me." The boy has now tied the verbal concept "authority" to the dimensions "old," "male," and "give orders" and has made the concept more accessible to consciousness.

Attributes of Concepts. There are four important qualities of a concept, apart from the meaning of its dimensions. These attributes are degree of abstraction, complexity, differentiation, and centrality of dimensions.

Degree of abstraction. Concepts differ in the nature of their dimensions. A concept whose dimensions are close to experience is said to be *concrete*. Hence real objects like dog, cat, house, and boy are represented by concrete concepts. Concepts whose dimensions refer to events that cannot be pointed to or experienced directly—like the concepts of intelligence, fairness, and corruption—are said to be *abstract*. The dimensions of concrete concepts are usually physical attributes one can see, hear, or touch. The dimensions of abstract concepts are often other concepts. The concept of intelligence, for example, rests on the dimensions of language proficiency, alertness, adaptability, and learning ability. Each of these four dimensions is itself an abstract concept resting on its own set of dimensions.

Complexity. Concepts also differ in the number of dimensions necessary to define them. Concepts that rest on many dimensions are regarded as more complex than those resting on only a few dimensions. The concept of society is complex, for it is defined by dimensions that include schools, courts, churches, customs, laws, and family structure, and each of these dimensions contains many dimensions within it. The concept of smoke, on the other hand, is simpler, for it rests on the three dimensions "wispy," "gray substance," and "rises in the air."

Differentiation. Concepts also differ in differentiation, or the degree to which the basic set of common qualities they represent can assume varied but related forms that describe slightly different versions of the idea. Thus the concept "rain" is not highly differentiated, for there are very few words in our language that describe different kinds of rain. Shower, rainstorm, and drizzle account for most of the forms of this event. Concepts like "hammer" and "bottle opener" are even less differentiated. However, the concept "house" is highly differentiated, for it can assume many different forms, from hut and cabin to bungalow and house to mansion and villa. Concepts that describe the appearance of things (adjectives) are also of varying differentiation. The concepts "attractive" and "bad" are highly differentiated, whereas the concepts "smooth" and "salty" are poorly differentiated, for we do not have many ways to describe differing degrees of smoothness to touch or saltiness of taste.

Generally, the concepts that are most significant to a culture are those that are most finely differentiated. Hence in our society the concept of property is captured by many related ideas, including land, money, furniture, stocks, bonds, cattle, and rights to an invention. The concept of inheritance, which is of considerably less significance to our society, has relatively few terms that distinguish among its forms.

Changes in the differentiation of a concept over time indicate the increasing or decreasing importance of the concept. Fifty years ago the concept "teacher" referred to a woman who taught in a public school. Today it can signify a professor, a speech therapist, a curriculum supervisor, a team-teacher, a teacher aide, or the man who arranges the program for a computer-instructed unit in arithmetic. The increased significance of drug experiences has led to a differentiation of the concept "high," which used to mean "drunk on alcohol" but now includes acid highs, speed highs, and pot highs.

Centrality of dimensions. Some concepts derive their essential meaning from one or two central dimensions; other concepts rest on a set of dimensions that are of equal importance in defining them. For example, the concept "infant" rests on the central dimension of age. Although size, type of food eaten, and crying are relevant dimensions, they are not critical, for infants differ in size, food intake, and irritability. But age is a critical dimension, for all infants are under eighteen months of age. The concept "living animal" by contrast rests equally on the dimensions: capacity to reproduce, to exchange oxygen, and to ingest food and egest waste. Each of these dimensions is of approximately equal significance in defining the concept.

These four qualities—abstraction, complexity, differentiation, and centrality of dimensions—can be applied to all concepts regardless of the meaning of their dimensions. But one particular pair of meanings, "good" and "bad," has a profound influence on the child's classification of his world. For the goodness or badness of an event is tied to the experience of pleasure or pain. Early in life the child learns to call objects and events that cause distress "bad" and those that bring pleasure "good." Food, warmth, mother, and ice cream are good; sickness, bruises, and spankings are bad. In his second and third years the child learns to attach guilt and anxiety to the dimension "bad" because violations of parental prohibitions are bad and because he is called bad by his parents if he disobeys their rules. Hence the unpleasant feelings of anxiety, fear of punishment, and eventually guilt are essential dimensions of the concept "bad," whereas feelings of contentment and security are essential to the concept "good." As indicated in the first part of this book, feelings are a major determinant of the importance of a motive in a person's mind, its place in the motive hierarchy. Similarly, the significance of a concept is governed by its relation to the dimensions of good and bad.

Concepts and Motives. It is likely that whether or not a concept is a moral standard or value is determined by its association with the good-bad dimension. A neutral concept is never a moral standard. The concepts "walk" and "run," which have no special relation to good or bad, are not standards; the concepts "steal" and "kill," which most children believe to be bad, are universal standards.

Since the child is motivated to make his behavior match his standards, motives can be viewed in part as concepts that are linked to good or bad. Consider the relatively complex concepts "friendship" and "book." Both are moderately differentiated, for there are many kinds of friendship (that of an acquaintance, friend, companion, intimate) and many kinds of books (textbook, notebook, novel, pamphlet). Both concepts rest on a central dimension (having someone's affection and trust; a set of printed pages). But the concept "friendship" is unequivocally regarded as good, whereas "book" is apt to be neutral. Thus the typical ten-year-old is motivated to have many friends but is usually not motivated to have many books.

Since a motive is a special kind of concept, it undergoes similar changes as the child matures. Most of the child's motives, like all his concepts, become more complex and more differentiated as he grows older. The concept of love and the motive for sexual stimulation are a good example. For the four-year-old, love is a relatively simple concept defined by affectionate relations between his parents and himself. There is little conceptual differentiation of degrees of love, and the child is as likely to say "I love you" when he is playing with his mother as when he is being tucked into bed and kissed good night. The child's concept of love rests centrally on feelings of pleasure and contentment derived from the relationship with his parents. Similarly, his sexual motivation has a central dimension of pleasant sensations from the genitals, with little differentiation of these feelings.

In adolescence major changes occur in both concepts. The concept of love takes on many dimensions, including relationships with parents, siblings, girlfriends, boyfriends, and occasionally teachers, and even feelings about hobbies, scenery, and favorite resorts. The increased complexity is accompanied by a dramatic change in differentiation, for there are many forms of love, which the adolescent designates by words like "love," "admiration," "attraction," and "desire." Sexual motivation undergoes a similar transformation. The adolescent's sexual motives rest not only on genital stimulation but on pictures, sounds, and thoughts. Sexual motivation becomes as much a state of mind as a distinct and urgent feeling. This differentiation of the concept of love and of the motive for sexual stimulation is extremely important for action. If the feeling is passion, then certain behaviors are more likely to occur than if the feeling is attraction. The popular songs of adolescence list the many forms sexual motivation can assume.

The increased complexity and differentiation of concepts and motives are partly responsible for the dramatic differences in personality structures among adults. Two-year-olds are probably more similar in the structure of their concepts than in their behavior. Twenty-year-olds, in contrast, have become socialized and are more similar in their behavior than in their ideas. Growing older is substituting internal complexity for external variety.

Relative and Absolute Concepts. One obstacle to the young child's effective use of concepts is his tendency to regard a concept as absolute rather than relative. The four-year-old, for example, learns the concept "dark" and regards it as descriptive of an absolute class of colors—black and other dark hues. The phrase "dark yellow" makes no sense to him, for dark signifies dark colors, not relative darkness. As a result, when the comparative forms of dark (darker, darkest) are introduced, he has no difficulty answering which is darker if red and black are presented to him but will appear confused if turquoise blue and sky blue are presented to him. He does not understand the question as a relative one. Similarly, the young child finds it difficult to understand the relative magnitude of numbers. He is told that 1, 2, and 3 are small numbers, that 99 and 100 are large numbers. But if he is asked which is the larger number of the pair 1 and 3, he may not understand the question.

It is not easy to teach the first grader to see both the absolute and relative qualities of concepts, for he must first be persuaded that the same concept can have two different meanings and must learn to use the concept from two different points of view. Perhaps the task can be lightened by attempting to persuade the child that familiar things like newspapers, oranges, and even himself can be regarded in different ways. Thus an orange is a good thing to eat but a bad ball to bounce; a newspaper is an easy thing to cut but a hard thing to mend trousers with. The child himself is many things at once: he is a boy and the son of his father; he is the smallest child in the family but the largest child in the classroom; he is cleanest when he is in the street but dirtiest when he has just returned from play; he is the heaviest child in the classroom but the lightest person in the family. By working with familiar ideas that the child can grasp easily, the teacher can gradually persuade the child of the important principle that *the quality of an object is relative to its context.* Some concepts do not have an absolute unchanging meaning. Appreciation of this idea is extremely important to the child's effective use of concepts.

There are two basic divisions of rules. First, all rules can be classified as nontransformational or transformational. A *nontransformational* rule states a simple relation between two concepts and is usually a statement about one or more of the dimensions of the concepts. For example, the rule "Water is wet" states that the concepts of water and wet are related—that is, one of the dimensions of water is the quality "wetness." The relation described by a nontransformational rule is always inherent in the meaning of the concepts. Consider the rule "Bombs are dangerous," which states a relation between the concepts of bomb and danger and describes the dimensions that the two concepts share. A bomb has many qualities, one of which is danger. Danger is a quality of many objects, one of which is a bomb. This rule does not require us to do anything in order to note the relation. It is present in the meaning of the concepts.

Now consider the rule "Place gunpowder and TNT in a metal case with a detonating cap and you have made a bomb." The relation among the concepts of gunpowder, TNT, metal case, and detonating cap is not clear until we act upon them and place them in special relation to one another. The concepts are related by this action. This type of rule, which involves a set of procedures that effect a relation, is said to be *transformational*. The procedures involved in making the relation are called *transformations*.

Second, all rules can be classified as informal or formal. *Informal* rules refer to an imperfect relation between two or more dimensions—that is, the dimensions are shared some of the time or even most of the time, but not all the time. "Candy is sweet" is an informal rule, for occasionally we find a candy that is sour. Most of our beliefs about the world are informal rules. "Snakes are dangerous," "Sand is dry," and "Men are tall" are informal rules that describe one of the dimensions of the concepts of snake, water, and man.

Formal rules state a relation between two dimensions that is always true and specifiable. "Oil floats on water" is a formal rule.

Similarly, the mathematical rule "6 times 11 is 66" states a fixed relation among the dimensions of the concepts "6" and "11" whenever the procedure of multiplication is applied to these concepts. There can be no quarrel with this relation.

There are therefore four major kinds of rules: informal, nontransformational ("Candy is sweet"); informal, transformational ("Melt chocolate and let it harden to make candy"); formal, nontransformational ("A triangle has three sides"); and formal, transformational ("6 times 11 is 66"). Most of our everyday thoughts are composed of informal, nontransformational rules; most of science is composed of formal, transformational rules. Each of the traditional subjects in school tends to emphasize one of these kinds of rules. Arithmetic and chemistry favor formal, transformational rules ("The area of a circle is πr^2," "$HCl + NaOH \rightarrow H_2O + NaCl$"). History and social studies focus on informal, nontransformational rules ("Wars cause inflation," "Industry develops near rivers"). Poetry uses informal, transformational rules in the construction of limericks and rhyming couplets.

Stages in the Acquisition of Rules. Some psychologists, among them Jerome Bruner, believe that the child gradually acquires more complex concepts and rules but that, in theory at least, no concept or rule is too difficult for a child to learn in some form at any age. Other psychologists, notably Jean Piaget, argue that some concepts and rules are inherently too difficult for the young child and that the child's mind must mature to a point where he can understand them. Consider the rule that a piece of clay does not change its weight or amount even though it changes its shape. This is a formal, nontransformational rule that in succinct form reads, "The amount of a substance remains constant despite changes in its form." The four-year-old does not possess this rule and it is very difficult to teach it to him. Yet by the time he is seven he knows the rule without ever being taught it.

How can we explain this phenomenon? Piaget's argument is that the four-year-old is simply not capable of mastering the rule. But there is also a second possibility—namely, that the child has learned an earlier rule that is difficult to replace. To the young child, the amount of an object or a substance is inextricably tied to its apparent height or size. Things that appear large or tall have more "stuff" than things that appear small. This is an informal, nontransformational rule that all young children possess. The advanced formal rule contradicts this earlier one, and the four-year-old does not easily give up a rule he has believed for several years. The seven-year-old firmly believes the advanced rule because he has acquired a new understanding of the word "amount." He has learned the arithmetic meaning of the concepts "more" and "less." Three apples remain three apples to him regardless of their size or arrangement because *three* is always *three*. The seven-year-old believes the formal rule as firmly as the four-year-old believes the informal rule that size and amount are somehow related. This change from an informal to a formal rule is one of the goals of arithmetic teaching.

The appearance of stages in the child's thought sometimes results from the fact that initially learned rules are difficult to replace. They stubbornly resist retirement, for they have been effective in the past. This simple maxim also holds for the larger entity called science. A scientific theory—which is an elaborate set of concepts and rules—is never replaced by criticism alone; it is replaced only by a better set of concepts and rules. A theory, like a rule, produces some order for the mind and remains strong until a better one appears. This sense of order derives from the fact that the central dimensions of concepts provide a frame of reference to which other qualities of experience can be related. A thought or perception is a quickly constructed process that has a primary point of reference— a benchmark, in a sense. As the mind gathers information, from the environment as well as from memory, in order to complete the construction, it automatically relates the new information to this basic point of reference.

Study the popular goblet illusion shown in Figure 1. If you focus your attention on the inner white space as the point of reference, the rest of the stimulus is automatically related to that point of focus and you are forced to see the goblet. You cannot help it. You relate the base of the goblet to that point of reference. But now shift your attention to the black part of the figure that defines the nose of the man. Notice how quickly your mind changes the direction of the relation. Now you relate the upper surface of the goblet to the lower part of the face. Notice how much easier it is to see the face if you use the nose rather than the forehead or chin as the point of reference.

The understanding of a sentence proceeds in a similar

FIGURE 1   The goblet illusion.

manner. Suppose you read or hear the sentence "Flying planes can be dangerous." If you focus on the word "flying" as an adjective describing planes, you understand the sentence to mean that planes in the air are potentially dangerous. However, if you focus on "flying" as a verb of action, the whole meaning of the sentence changes and it is the act of flying planes that is potentially dangerous. Once a point of reference is decided—and it is decided automatically—there is an immediate tendency to relate all other information to it.

This phenomenon has relevance for the more complicated processes of motivation and emotion. For example, suppose a man is sitting next to an attractive woman on an airplane and the woman suddenly smiles at him after an hour of conversation. How is this piece of information to be perceived? How is the man to relate that simple event to his ongoing understanding of his past interaction with the woman? If he takes his immediately preceding statement as the point of reference, he will try to relate the woman's smile to its content and style. If that construction makes sense, he will probably accept it as valid. However, if the man relates the smile to his conception of the woman's motives—say, that he believes she is trying to exploit him—the smile will be viewed as strengthening that initial view. Or the man may have decided earlier that he was going to seduce the woman and so interprets her smile as evidence that he is succeeding.

Thus the man can interpret the woman's smile in at least three different ways; he can insert it into one of three different constructions. Actually, all three interpretations might be incorrect. The woman might have smiled because, at that moment, she thought of an interaction that occurred with her child at breakfast the previous day. The interpretation of experience is a little like making constructions from wet sand on a summer beach. Children can use it to make castles, blankets for their fathers, or cupcakes.

This view of perception of the external world is different from the one that has been prevalent in American psychology. The traditional view has conceived of a set of definite stimuli impinging upon a person and forcing him to experience specific events. The image is one of Gulliver tied down by Lilliputians who are shooting "stimulus" arrows at him. The view of perception presented here suggests a different image, that of Gulliver up and about, wandering through the land examining strange events—rocks, plants, and people—and trying to understand the new country by relating what he perceives to what he knows. If he does not actively examine a small yellow pebble, it has little power to influence him. More generally, if man does not selectively focus his attention on an aspect of his environment, he is usually uninfluenced by it. Obviously, both images are a little too extreme, for even a tied-down Gulliver can duck some arrows; he is not completely helpless. And an active, walking Gulliver will be unable to avoid turning around if he hears a loud explosion; he is not completely free. But most of the time we are forced neither to "duck" experience nor to interrupt an ongoing activity because of an intense and unexpected intrusion. Most of the day we are browsers in a large curiosity shop in which the goods are reflected in a distorting mirror and we must decide what they are and whether we want them.

IMPLICATIONS FOR THE TEACHER

The teacher should systematically attempt an analysis of the major concepts she presents in class. All concepts differ in abstractness, complexity, differentiation, and centrality of dimensions, and in their relation to the concepts of good and bad. The teacher should introduce concepts to students in terms of these attributes and should try to work first with those dimensions that the child already knows. Consider the concept of school. It is relatively simple, for it rests on the primary dimension "learn skills." Secondary dimensions like age of students and the specific place where the learning occurs are less central to the meaning of school. In addition, there is some differentiation of the concept, for there are private schools, public schools, parochial schools, boarding schools, and schools for the emotionally disturbed. Finally, the concept of school seems moderately associated with good and bad.

In contrast, the concept of science is more abstract and more complex. It is also moderately differentiated, for there are natural science, social science, political science, and physical science. The dimensions of science include explanation of nature, experimentation, observation, prediction of future events, control of nature, and laboratories. The junior high school teacher might ask her students which of these dimensions is most central to the concept of science. Hopefully, the consensus of the class will be that explanation of nature is central. The students' evaluation of science as good or bad is likely to depend on their attitudes toward the social consequences of discovery and the control of human beings.

The teacher may also find it useful to compare similar concepts like boy and man, ocean and sea, or fruit and vegetable and ask the class to generate the central dimensions of each concept. The teacher can make a game of asking the class to suggest concepts that have the *most* or the *fewest* dimensions, or to analyze the central dimensions of concepts like beauty, war, and love and compare their relation to the dimensions of good and bad. Student disagreement on the central dimensions of concepts can provide the teacher with the opportunity to point out that people have different points of view on many popular issues. Lively class discussion can be generated by analysis of the critical dimensions of concepts, for every child would have to examine his own understanding of each concept.

The teacher should always analyze the concepts that are part of her lesson before giving her presentation. This preparation will help her to appreciate the abstractness, complexity, differentiation, and centrality of dimensions of the concepts she is presenting. The teacher who gains competence at this kind of analysis will feel in greater control of her presentations and more confident of her ability and will be in a better position to diagnose learning blocks when they occur. The teacher will also find it helpful before presenting a lesson to assess the degree to which the children in her class have similar views of a particular concept. For example, suppose the second-grade lesson is magnetism. The teacher might ask several children of different abilities to describe what they understand this concept to mean—to list the dimensions of magnetism—and to give their view of the centrality of each dimension. After writing their responses on the blackboard, the teacher can initiate a short class discussion to reveal the extent of class agreement, disagreement, or confusion about the concept. The teacher will then have a rough conception of the students' understanding of magnetism and can use this information to guide her presentation.

Most second-grade children have difficulty understanding the meaning of speed. The teacher may find it helpful to present this notion as a relation between the central dimensions of the concepts "time" and "distance." For example, if the teacher presents the basic dimension of distance as "the space between two lines" and the basic dimension of time as "the number of ticks on a clock," she can then introduce speed as "the number of spaces covered per tick." Teaching the relative sizes of countries can be approached by a set of comparisons. The teacher might start with a concept whose size is known—for example, the size of a familiar town or the time required to travel a certain known distance. The teacher can then "build up" the concept of relative size by presenting countries as multiples of that familiar unit. This is the strategy implied in the use of light years to designate the distance of stars from the earth.

The teaching of the concept of time should involve the child's view of its central dimensions, not necessarily the standard dimensions of hours and seconds. Since time for the young child is usually divided into "school time" and "after-school time," the teacher should initially compare Saturdays and Sundays with the other five days of the week. Other major features of time for the young child are "before lunch" and "after lunch" and "night" and "day." All time concepts should be introduced by these dimensions, for they are most meaningful to the very young child.

For example, the monthly calendar, which is a confusing object to most children, should be initially presented in terms of time units that the child understands. The teacher might find it helpful to use a seven-day blackboard calendar in which the basic distinction is between "school days" and "no-school days." Such a calendar should have seven boxes, with the initial letter for the day of the week written over each box, beginning with Saturday and Sunday on the left and ending with Friday on the right. This seven-day rectangle should be large and clear and presented at the child's eye level. On Monday the teacher should draw the calendar on the board and point out that the children have been home and away from school for two days, called the "no-school days." These days should be marked with an X in colored chalk. The teacher should then point to the third box and explain that it stands for a particular day and should mark this box with a different color chalk. Each day the next box should be marked with the color chalk for school days, and at the end of the week the calendar should be erased. This procedure should be followed for four weeks, with the teacher supervising the marking of each day and asking the children which color chalk to use, the chalk for no-school days or the chalk for school days. After the children have learned the concept of a week and the distinction between school days and no-school days, the weeks can be cumulated on a monthly calendar. Now the teacher leaves the seven-day calendar on the blackboard rather than erasing it. The following Monday a second row of seven boxes is drawn beneath the first; and so on until the month is completed. (See Gotkin, 1967.)

Teaching is like a doctor's prescription; it should be based on a careful diagnosis of the patient's state. There is enormous benefit to be gained from continual class analysis of the dimensions of concepts and from diagnosis of each child's state of understanding. After several months the young child will get into the habit of automatically asking himself about the central dimensions of new concepts. This is a major dividend, for the child will have acquired a tool for intellectual analysis of new ideas as well as for better understanding of existing ones. Learning will become less mechanical and more meaningful, and the child will be prepared to note the relations among different concepts.

The central implication of this discussion is that the teacher should not teach a rule before she is moderately certain the child understands the concepts it involves. Curriculum units in social studies or history often teach rules about the functions of nations and cities to children who do not understand the central dimensions of these concepts. For example, a child cannot appreciate the famous rule "Taxation without representation is tyranny" unless he understands the meaning of the three basic concepts in it. A concept should be presented initially in its simple form, with complexity introduced gradually. The concept of number should be introduced initially as a set of objects, for "set" is a central dimension of number. Only after this dimension is understood should the teacher introduce the dimensions that involve the transformational rules on numbers called addition, subtraction, multiplication, and division. The teacher might also introduce the idea that a whole number can imply a range, that the number 2 can be viewed as lying between 1.5 and 2.5. Once the child understands the concept of range, the teacher can discuss the notion of estimation of a number value. She should emphasize differences in the size of the number field—single digits 0–9, versus double digits 10–99, and so on—and frequently compare these classes. The teacher should continually contrast addition and subtraction on the same pairs of numbers, thereby sharpening the child's appreciation of these two rules. When arithmetic word problems are introduced, she should present a series of lessons that teach the child which phrases of word problems are critical. The child should be taught to attack problems step by step, to ask himself if a difference, a sum, or a product is involved in each case. Consider the problem "If John had 10 cows and Paul had 40 cows, how many more cows did John have than Paul?" The child should be taught to ask himself immediately, "Is this a difference or a sum? Are the units the same or different?"

Some rules are harder to learn than others because the concepts they involve are more difficult to understand. The rule for the circumference or area of a circle is easier to learn than the rule for the volume of a sphere, and the typical strategy of postponing three-dimensional measurement until the child has understood two-dimensional measurement is reasonable. As the child learns to read, he constructs his own informal set of rules, which he rarely makes explicit. He comes to expect a noun when he sees an adjective of description, to expect a verb of action when he sees an animal or human subject, and to expect an adverb of location when he sees the word "go." Possession of these rules makes reading easier and faster. The controversy surrounding the value of phonic versus whole-word teaching is easily resolved once one recognizes that the phonic approach teaches a useful set of rules. The whole-word method does not supply the six-year-old with many useful rules to apply to new words. The child's classroom motivation might be improved if the teacher structured the reading task as a game in which the child had to discover the basic rules.

Indeed, the entire educational enterprise should be so structured. The world of experience, like the printed page, is a puzzle that the child has to assemble in a way that makes sense to him. In order to solve the puzzle he must have the basic pieces, which are the cognitive structures just considered. He also needs to know how to put the pieces together. This function is described by the cognitive processes, to which we now turn our attention.

The Processes of Thought

THE NATURE OF THE COGNITIVE PROCESSES

Cognitive processes—or more simply, thought—can be divided into two major types. In *undirected thought,* the mind is free of the burden of solving any problem and can wander in a variety of directions, skipping abruptly from idea to idea. Daydreams and the easy flow of ideas that occur when one is watching snow fall or upon waking in the morning are the best examples of undirected thought. It is difficult to study this important phenomenon because psychologists do not know how to probe the private nature of undirected thought without seriously disturbing it. If you ask a person to report his free associations—the thoughts that happen to be running through his mind—the question abruptly changes the fluid nature of his thinking, and what was undirected suddenly becomes directed.

The child who is asked a question has a problem to solve. As a result, he automatically attempts to organize a logical, coherent, and socially acceptable report of his thoughts. The request to report what he is thinking changes the nature of his thoughts and his subsequent reply will not contain the disorder or lack of logic that is often characteristic of undirected cognition. Thus *directed thought* involves all the cognitive processes that come into play when the child attempts to solve a problem, whether it is a problem he had set for himself or one that a teacher or parent has presented to him.

When the child's thought is directed he is usually faced with a problem that he believes can be solved, and he knows when he has arrived at the solution.

The problem-solving process typically follows the following sequence. First, the child must comprehend the problem, whether it is presented orally or in written form. Next, he must hold the elements of the problem in his memory while he generates possible solutions. The child must then evaluate his understanding of the problem and the adequacy of his hypotheses. Finally, he must choose the best hypothesis and implement it. Under special circumstances, the child must also report the answer to someone. Thus the major processes in problem-solving are comprehension, memory, generation of ideas, evaluation of ideas, implementation, and occasionally public report. Each of these processes is considered in detail below.

It is helpful to keep in mind in the following pages the general changes that occur over the period three through twelve years of age. The child's supply of schemata, images, symbols, concepts, and rules becomes richer and undergoes continual reorganization as a function of experience. The child becomes concerned with the degree of accord between his ideas and those of others, and he becomes more anxious about making mistakes. In addition, his ability to remember new facts and to recall old ones improves dramatically. Perhaps most important, his conception of problems and the rules he activates to solve them gradually approach those of the adult.

PERCEPTION AND INTERPRETATION

The first process in problem-solving is the accurate perception and interpretation of the problem. Although children always spontaneously interpret events around them, the form of their interpretations changes with age. The infant or very young child usually translates experience into schemata or images, whereas the older child is likely to rely on symbols and concepts. Consider the following stimulus, which is not a perfect circle but an ellipse: ⬭
A ten-month-old child is likely to represent this figure as a schema that is faithful to the shape of the stimulus. A six-year-old child is likely to represent such an event symbolically or conceptually and might say, "It looks like a ball." But if asked to select an identical

figure from a set of similar ones, he might make an error that revealed he actually perceived it as a ball or a perfect circle; and if asked to reproduce the figure, he might draw a circle rather than an ellipse.

The Preference for Single Strategies of Interpretation. Children as well as adults have a strong tendency to rely on the same set of units to interpret experience, a type of inflexibility that tempts them to view a variety of situations or problems in a "preferred" way. A child may be in the habit of regarding objects in terms of their functions rather than as members of certain conceptual classes. Foods are "things to eat" rather than fruits, vegetables, or cereals; animals are "things that bite" rather than dogs, cows, or sheep.

This preference for a single strategy of interpreting experience can lead to difficulty when the teacher introduces a new curriculum aid that forces the child to deal with a particular idea or object in a new way. For example, some teachers use Cuisenaire rods to teach first graders about numbers and the simple rules of arithmetic. The rods are wooden sticks of different colors. The number *1* is represented by a colored stick one unit long; the number 2 is represented by a stick of a different color, twice as long as the one-unit stick; and so on. The advantage of this method of teaching numbers is that it gives the young child a concrete way to represent the concept of number as a symbolic amount. Numbers are a new symbol for the child, and the stimulus "1 + 1 = □" is a new event to be understood. However, if the child learns to represent numbers as rods of different lengths and colors, he may develop a strong tendency to translate *all* numbers and number problems into schemata or images of these rods. This tendency can be troublesome when long division or multiplication problems are introduced in later grades. The young child should probably be weaned from the Cuisenaire representation of numbers before he comes to rely too strongly on it and becomes unable to shift to a new system. The child should always be given practice with different ways to interpret or deal with school materials.

Perception and Attention to Distinctive Elements. An event is defined by its distinctive elements. For a face, the arrangement of the eyes is distinctive; for an animal, the legs are distinctive;

for a letter, a break in the continuity of a line is distinctive. The young child is more likely to regard a break in a straight line or a circle as a distinctive characteristic of a letter than a change in the perspective of the figure. Thus the capital letter *B* is easily perceived as different from the number 8 because of the relation between the straight and curved lines. Although the letter *B* in perspective looks like the numeral 8, it is readily seen as a letter, not a number, because it preserves the relation between the straight and curved lines. Professor E. J. Gibson of Cornell University showed preschool and school-age children novel line designs, like those illustrated in Figure 2. The children were also shown a row of similar designs from which they were asked to select one that was exactly like a single design on top. The children's responses indicated that they did not notice changes in perspective, for they often regarded ⊥ as similar to ⊥ . However, they rarely regarded ⊥ as similar to ± . The "break" between the vertical and the horizontal was an important feature of the stimulus. Curved and straight lines were also significant features to the children, for they were not likely to regard ⊥ or ⊥ as similar to ⊥ Thus open versus closed (continuity of line) and curved versus straight are distinctive elements of line designs for children.

We may wonder whether the young child naturally makes these distinctions or whether he is led to do so by his knowledge of letters, which are distinguished by the same features. For example, the pairs *O* versus *C*, *O* versus *G*, and *R* versus *B* are differentiated

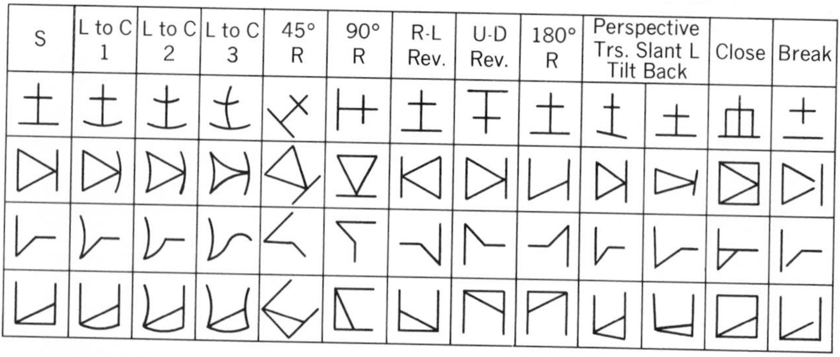

S	L to C 1	L to C 2	L to C 3	45° R	90° R	R-L Rev.	U-D Rev.	180° R	Perspective Trs. Slant L Tilt Back	Close	Break

FIGURE 2 Designs used in studies of perceptual discrimination.

in part because one letter has a break and the other does not. The pairs *D* versus *O*, *U* versus *V*, and *S* versus *Z* are differentiated by the fact that one letter has a curved dimension and the other a straight-line dimension. (See Gibson, 1963.) But are letters themselves easy to distinguish because the child naturally makes the open-closed and curved-straight distinctions or because he has already acquired some familiarity with letters? We do not know. Nonetheless, since the first-grade child is attracted to these features, the teacher should exploit this fact.

Letters of the alphabet are usually taught sequentially—*a, b, c, d,* and so on—but should perhaps be taught in pairs that contrast distinctive elements, such as *z* versus *n, c* versus *o, c* versus *d, m* versus *w, r* versus *k, u* versus *v,* and *n* versus *m.* The distinctive elements in words are the letter sequences, and the teacher should contrast pairs like *tar* versus *rat, passes* versus *passed,* and *go* versus *going.* As the child becomes a more proficient reader, the distinctive units become larger. If he sees the three letters *-ing* at the end of a word, he treats them as a unit with a characteristic sound and implied meaning. These rules of reading are learned quickly, and as the child masters them his reading speed improves, for he does not have to pause to analyze individual letters in new words. If he comes across the word "substitutions" in the sentence "The coach wished he could have more substitutions in the football game," it is likely that all he would have to see in order to comprehend the meaning would be *sub . . . tu . . ons.* The three groups of letters and the two spaces in between should probably be sufficient for correct recognition.

Perception and Attention to Several Elements.   The young child has difficulty focusing attention on more than one event at a time. If he tries to listen to or watch many things at once, he often becomes confused. Hence an adult can better understand two simultaneous utterances than a seven-year-old. Since it is likely that the adult can perceive only one word at a time, he must be constructing what is being said by each speaker from his knowledge of language. Consider the following pair of sentences:

Speaker A:	[I said]	that he	[better leave]	at once.
Speaker B:	Why don't	[you have]	a cold	[drink now]?

Suppose that the bracketed words are those heard by the listener. Most adults can infer the meanings of both sentences even though they hear only half the words in each. The young child does not have such sophisticated language skill. He is less familiar with word sequences and therefore has a more difficult time making sentence constructions.

The teacher should appreciate this limitation in the young child and should always make sure that she has every child's attention during instruction. A good way to accomplish this goal is to have more adults in the classroom, especially during the primary grades, when children are easily distracted. Ideally, reading instruction should be between one adult and two or three children. Since it is impossible to have half a dozen certified teachers in every primary grade—the cost is prohibitive—many schools use paraprofessionals—neighborhood mothers and high school students. The latter group is an excellent reservoir of needed talent and help. The majority of high school students are eager to give something of value to the community, and many would love to be assigned a few first-grade children to tutor for one hour three times a week. A personal relationship would be established between the child and his adolescent "teacher" and the child's motivation should blossom.

Many school systems experimenting with such a plan have reported positively on its potential. This plan should be national in scope. The classroom teacher cannot hold the attention of thirty seven-year-olds for more than a few minutes, and she spends most of her day disciplining. Thus the use of mothers and high school students is one of the most important, and potentially beneficial, changes in public education in a century. It is surprising that we did not think of it earlier.

The Role of Expectancy in Interpretation. The child's interpretation of experience is related to what he anticipates. If a child knows what he is about to see or hear, he can better prepare himself for the event. Such preparation makes his perceptions more accurate. In one study, school-age children (from kindergarten and grades two, four, and six) were asked to listen to and repeat two-word phrases spoken by a man's voice and a woman's voice. The voices came simultaneously from two loudspeakers, one marked with the picture of a man and the other with a picture of a woman. When the child was to report the words spoken by the man's voice, the man's picture was lighted; when the child was to report the words spoken by the woman, her picture was lighted. On some trials the picture of the man or woman was lighted *before* the voices spoke—that is, the child was given a signal as to which voice to listen to. On other trials the picture was lighted *after* the voices spoke. When the child was told which voice to listen to *before* the voices spoke, his performance was better than when he was told after the voice spoke. (Maccoby, 1967.)

Developmental Changes in Sustained Attention. Between five and seven years of age a dramatic improvement takes place in the quality of the child's intellectual performance, particularly on problems that require focused attention. This developmental change seems to occur not only for American children but for children in cultures less technical than the United States. Many psychologists report that the child under five years of age is easily distracted and has difficulty focusing his attention for a long time on a problem or an instruction. After seven years of age the child's distractability seems repaired. This improvement in quality of attention and subsequent thought may be due to biological changes in the central nervous system. It is possible that an important reorganization of the central nervous system occurs between five and seven years of age and is partly responsible for the increase in the child's capacity to devote prolonged attention to problems. (White, 1968.)

Some first-grade children will have already made the transition to the more mature stage and are able to concentrate for long periods of time. Others are not. The teacher should determine which children in her class have this capacity and should adjust her demands accordingly. A good technique to aid the teacher in this diagnosis is a recall test. The first-grade child who cannot recall a sequence of four numbers may not have passed through the critical stage when sustained attention suddenly becomes less of a burden.

MEMORY

Memory is the elusive process that permits us to store perceived experience in order to recall the past. For a number of years many psychologists believed that all experience that was perceived was registered somewhere in the brain and was therefore potentially capable of being remembered. If a man could not remember some scene or person he had encountered a week earlier, it was assumed that the fault lay with his inability to recall the event rather than with its initial registration.

We now believe that there are at least two distinct memory processes, called *short-term* and *long-term memory*. The information in short-term memory is available for only a few seconds and rarely for more than half a minute. The ease with which we forget the name of a new acquaintance or a telephone number after we have dialed it is a common example of short-term memory. A person must make a special effort to place a new experience in long-term memory. If he does not, some or all of that information will be lost and unavailable at a later time.

Measuring Memory. The content of a child's memory is usually measured in one of two ways. The child is asked either to *recall* what he saw or heard or to *recognize* it. In a recall test, the child must search his memory for the missing idea and retrieve all the necessary information; he is given no hints. When he is asked to define a word or remember a historical date, he must try to recall it from memory. In a recognition test, the child is given both the correct and incorrect information and must select the fact that he believes is desired. It should be obvious that there will be a significant difference in the child's ability to recognize an event and his ability to recall it. But this difference is much more dramatic in young children than in older ones. If a ten-year-old is shown a group of twelve pictures, he will usually be able to recall seven or eight of them and recognize all twelve. Thus his recall is about 30 percent poorer than his recognition. But if a four-year-old is shown the pictures, he will be able to recall only three of them and recognize all twelve. The young child's recall is 75 percent poorer than his recognition. This difference becomes more profound as the number of pictures is increased. If the ten-year-old is shown fifty pictures, he will recognize forty-eight of them and recall about fifteen. The four-year-old is likely to recognize forty-five pictures but recall less than five.

The subtle sensation that one has heard or seen an event in

the past is a common experience. The ability to reconstruct the event is another matter. Recalling an event often requires finding a label or verbal description for it. In addition, recall is extremely vulnerable to interference and is influenced by the context in which the memory search occurs. Think of the many times you had a name on the tip of your tongue but were unable to recall it. If someone had said the name, you would have recognized at once that it was correct.

The teacher should realize that recognition tests are dramatically more sensitive indexes of how much a child knows than recall tests. The recall test is useful, however, in assessing how firmly a fact is known. Each strategy has its place, depending upon what the teacher wants to measure. If she wants to determine quickly whether a second-grade child has learned a lesson on subtraction, she should administer a recognition test, in which the child must state if certain answers are correct or incorrect. If the teacher wants to know how well the lesson has been learned, she should administer a recall test, in which the child is asked to perform the operations.

Bases for Differences in Memory. Children under six or seven years of age can hold only a few words or ideas in their mind when someone is speaking to them and have greater difficulty than preadolescents in recalling events that happened hours, days, or weeks earlier. There are two major reasons the young child displays a poorer memory. First, the child has a less adequate set of cognitive units—schemata, images, symbols, concepts, and rules—to label incoming information. Language is one of the essential "glues" of thought. The labeling of an event helps the child to hold it in memory longer because the act of naming is associated with increased attention to the event. Second, the young child has not yet learned—or does not wish to use—the device of *rehearsal*. He does not spontaneously repeat events to himself in order to hold them in memory for later retrieval. He ambles through experience and does not consciously try to retain significant portions of it. It does not occur to him that silent rehearsal has any value. Perhaps this reluctance or inability to rehearse means that the young child has not yet learned that some of his "troubles" are due to a failure of memory. A child who wanders away from his mother in a department store and becomes frightened is not likely to attribute this trauma to the fact that he did not stop to remember where his mother was standing when he left her.

The primary-grade teacher should encourage rehearsal and initiate exercises that teach the young child memory tricks—techniques of grouping words and ideas, efficient ways to rehearse information, and strategies of free associating to material that must be recalled later. These exercises should make the child constructively conscious of his ability to store information and should persuade him of his power to shape and control his mental activity.

Differences in quality of memory among children of the same age are often due to differences in degree of anxiety. Anxiety is a major cause of memory difficulties because it interferes with focused attention. Anxious children generally show poor recall ability because the feelings and thoughts that comprise anxiety are distracting and deflect attention from the information to be remembered. In a recent study, a group of third-grade boys was made anxious as a result of being unable to solve a problem; a second group was given information that enabled them to succeed with the problem; and a third group was not given the problem. Each child was then read a short story and asked to recall as much of it as possible. The group that had been made anxious displayed the poorest memory for the story. (Messer, 1968.)

Finally, quality of memory depends on motivation. Is the child motivated to retrieve knowledge or does he stop searching after the first layer of information has been remembered? The retrieval of information from memory requires effort, and the child who is motivated to work longer is likely to ferret out more information.

Aiding Memory. It takes a little time to transfer information to long-term memory. The child needs time to synthesize what he has perceived, and it is wise to pace the delivery of information. On occasion, delaying the answer leads to better subsequent test performance than giving the child the answer immediately. Presumably, this effect occurs because the delay gives the child time to organize the mental activity he has just completed. The teacher should be aware of what segments of knowledge she wants the child to absorb and should pause in her delivery of information at critical points in order to promote proper synthesis. One disadvantage of some teaching-machine programs is that they do not allow sufficient time for synthesis, for quiet reflection and the savoring of an answer. (This problem is discussed in greater detail below.)

Information is also more likely to be recalled if it is presented in several modalities—auditory, visual, tactual, and even olfactory when feasible. The use of multimodal representations increases the number of distinctive elements in the learning experience and can therefore help the child to retrieve the information later. For example, in reading exercises the teacher can present not only actual objects but clay, sandpaper, or flannel representations of letters and simple words. The opportunity to feel as well as see the letters *j-u-m-p* should help the child to register the distinctive features of this word.

Memory is one of the most important processes in thought, but it is also the most elusive. Its capacity for holding information is enormous, yet it is fragile and vulnerable to the slightest interference. It is powerful, yet easily disturbed. Memory is sustained by new schemata, symbols, and concepts that facilitate its growth. Its enemies are distraction, anxiety, and lack of motivation. Memory is continually active; it reorganizes segments of knowledge into a more meaningful system. The teacher must help the child learn how to place new knowledge in memory and to search his memory store; above all, she must keep distraction and anxiety low.

GENERATION OF IDEAS

The third process in problem-solving is the generation of possible solutions, the development of alternate ways to solve a problem. In order to generate good ideas the child must possess the right set of schemata, images, symbols, and rules, must be free of the fear of making a mistake, and must have that more mystical ingredient called insight. The child is motivated to seek solutions whenever he encounters a situation that he does not understand or a problem for which he does not have an immediate answer. Every new event creates a state of uncertainty in the young child, for he does not have an easy rule or concept to explain the event and to persuade him that he understands why it occurred. The child wants to resolve this uncertainty; he wants to understand. In order to find an answer he must dip into his reservoir of knowledge and search for structures that will enable him to create an explanation.

How does the child know when he has explained a strange event or solved a problem? How does he know when he is right? A seven-year-old sees his mother weeping and has never seen her crying before. The event is discrepant and stirs him to try to account for it. He automatically thinks of the conditions that make *him* cry—physical pain, fear, and loneliness. He checks the plausibility of each of these as a cause of his mother's action. The child rejects the fear interpretation because it contradicts another rule he believes more firmly—namely, that adults are never afraid. He rejects the loneliness hypothesis for the same reason. But he knows that adults are capable of feeling pain and so decides that this interpretation is correct. He is satisfied.

This simple example illustrates the three steps involved in the generation of any explanation:

1. The child searches his set of mental structures, especially his concepts and rules, for possible causes of an event that he does not immediately understand and generates several possible explanations.
2. The child checks each hypothesis for consistency with his older rules about the event. If an explanation contradicts an older rule, which the child believes more strongly, he is likely to reject the new interpretation.
3. If the child finds an explanation that both matches his experience and does not contradict an older rule, he will probably accept it as correct.

Obstacles to the Generation of Ideas.   There are four major obstacles to the generation of new explanations to problems. First, a child may be unable to find a new explanation because he does not understand the nature of the problem. For example, children under ten years of age usually have difficulty reasoning about situations that involve hypothetical events. Consider the following problem: "A three-headed fish flew 4 miles one day and 3 miles the next day. How many miles did the fish fly all together?" The six-year-old may refuse to work at this problem and may rationalize his refractory attitude by reminding the interrogator that there are no three-headed fish, and that fish can't fly anyway. The twelve-year-old is able to accept this hypothetical state of affairs and will work at the problem.

A second obstacle to the generation of possible explanations is lack of an appropriate set of rules or ideas. The life experiences of a child often determine whether or not he will possess the ideas needed to solve a problem. Suppose the following problem were posed to a group of second graders in rural Alabama and to another group in New York City: "A man is in a log cabin on a cold, windy night. All he has with him are some old newspapers and a pot of glue. What should he do to keep warm?" The solutions generated by each child can be traced to his life experiences. The lower-class rural child is more likely than the urban one to suggest that the newspapers be glued against the window to keep out the wind, for he has seen this technique used with profit. This suggestion is less likely to come from the urban child because, in his experience, windows are usually intact, even in an urban slum.

A third obstacle to the generation of good ideas is the possession of a firmly held rule that contradicts a possible explanation. For example, a fifth-grade teacher asks her class why some knights joined the Crusades, what their reasons were for traveling thousands of miles from their homes. The child who believes that the Crusaders were good Christians would not be likely to generate the suggestion that a desire for property was a motive because this idea contradicts a strongly held existing rule.

A final obstacle to the generation of good ideas is fear of making a mistake. The typical school-age child is not only afraid of social criticism for making an error; he also has self-generated feelings of condemnation for violating his own standards of competence. The easiest and most common response the child makes to fear of error is withdrawal from the task or, if the fear is mild, inhibition about offering answers that he is unsure of. Every teacher recognizes this syndrome, for each class has a few children who are intelligent but overly inhibited. They know more than they are saying. They censor good ideas because they would rather avoid making a mistake than experience the joy of success. The teacher should reduce these fears by encouraging guessing and by convincing the child that honest error is no sin, that approximations are better than no response, and that any attempt is better than withdrawal.

The conditions that stifle the generation of ideas change their relative power at different points in the life span. Young children usually fail to generate good ideas because they fear social criticism; most adults fail because they hold a set of older rules about a phenomenon that forces them to reject an insightful solution. Thus most nineteenth-century scientists rejected Darwin's evolutionary ideas and Freud's notion of the unconscious because these concepts violated their fundamental beliefs about nature and people.

This phenomenon has been captured in the laboratory. In one study, ten college students were isolated in a room and given a difficult problem to solve. The students were told that the task was to be a cooperative game: if they solved the problem together they would all receive an appropriate award, but there would be no reward for an individual solution. The group worked all morning without success. After lunch, one member of the group, an accomplice of the experimenter, wrote out the correct solution. Most of the students rejected it, even though, with study, they would have realized that it was correct. Each student became convinced during the long morning that the problem could not be solved, and having arrived at that belief, found it difficult to acknowledge that anyone was able to do so. (Ratoosh, 1966.)

In a study of creativity and personality, a group of fifth-grade girls was given standard tests of intelligence and tests of creativity, in which they were asked to generate unusual ideas. The girls who displayed both high intelligence and high creativity on the tests were self-confident in school and popular with their friends. The girls who displayed high intelligence but low creativity were sought out by others but often failed to respond to these overtures because of social cautiousness. (Wallach and Kogan, 1965.) Thus the creative child is more willing to take a chance, to risk offering a strange idea, for he has a more permissive attitude toward possible error.

An idea that is original but unrelated to a problem is not necessarily creative. If this book were written in Gaelic and printed upside down, it would be original but obviously not creative. A creative idea derives from a set of beliefs about a problem and improves upon them. A creative idea never stands alone, unrelated to other, earlier solutions. Hence first-grade children are not likely to be creative, for they do not have a rich reservoir of ideas from which they might synthesize unusually good solutions to problems. This is not to say that we should belittle novelty or originality in young children; rather, we should not mistake the young child's originality for those products we call creative in the adolescent and adult.

"Learning to Learn." The child's reservoir of ideas is organized in packages for particular problems. As a result, some solution

hypotheses are always the first ones tried for specific kinds of problems. For example, second graders feel that if a teacher gives them a problem with two numbers, they are supposed either to add or to subtract them. These are the two strongest hypotheses for the second grader and the ones he will try first. The automatic tendency to use a particular rule for certain problems is a kind of mental set. Young children take longer to discard old, established mental sets than young adults. The phrase "learning to learn" refers to the child's readiness to discard old approaches to a problem and to adopt a more effective method of attack. The child who has "learned to learn" analyzes a particular kind of problem in a flexible manner, attends to its relevant aspects, and discards inefficient hypotheses. In essence, the child has learned a general approach to a specific class of problems. If a person played "Twenty Questions" each day for thirty days, the quality of his questions would improve dramatically, even though the specific person or object he was trying to guess changed each day. Practice would have taught him how to ask better questions and to avoid asking questions that do not give much information.

IMPLICATIONS FOR THE TEACHER

The school tries to teach the child new symbols, concepts, and rules and to help him learn how to generate relevant ideas when he is faced with a problem. The second task is considerably more difficult than the first. The ten-year-old's head is stuffed with bits of knowledge in some form of organization, but the child's rules and concepts tend to be initially restrictive, limited to the materials that were used to teach him the concepts in the first place. The teacher should not be frustrated when the child does not apply or use a concept or rule in a situation different from the one in which he originally acquired it. The child is taught, for example, that the associative law allows him to translate $9(6x + 8)$ to $54x + 72$. But many children will not know what to do with the expression $x(9y + 8)$. They have learned the associative law with an integer outside the parentheses, and they do not realize that the same rule is applicable when the integer is replaced by a variable.

The question of generalization of rules has been the subject of much controversy in education. In the 1930's many educators believed in the power of "transfer of training" and used this idea to defend the teaching of many subjects, including Latin and Greek. The assumption was that the rules of word construction and syntax learned in Latin could be generalized to English and could help the student in his composition. The research on this issue is generally negative and disheartening. Most children learn rules and concepts to the specific materials they encounter and do not easily retrieve them when they are applicable to a new problem. It is useful therefore in teaching concepts and rules to present a broad array of examples during the initial tutoring of the idea. For example, in discussing the causes of the American Civil War, the teacher should consider the parallels with many other wars—domestic and foreign, recent and ancient—and should point out the similarities among them. In many school systems, the fifth-grade child learns about the American Revolutionary War, the sixth-grade child about the American Civil War, the eighth-grade child about the Crusades, and the tenth-grade child about World War I. It would be better to have a social studies unit on "Wars and Their Causes" that pointed out the dimensions common to all wars. The child should be taught the important principle that a conflict of interest between two powerful groups is present prior to every war, so that when he is asked about the cause of the Spanish-American War he need not search his mind for the particular precipitating incident but can immediately ask himself, "Who were the conflicting parties and what were the central disagreements?"

This principle is maximally useful in the teaching of natural science in junior high school and high school, for there are a large number of specific concepts to be learned in the content areas of chemistry, biology, and physics. Since the general concepts of cause, effect, mechanism of change, and equilibrium are applicable to each of these sciences, it would be wise to present them first, giving examples from all three disciplines. Thus, when the adolescent thinks about the term "equilibrium," he will imagine not only a chemist's beaker but a cell membrane and a heat sink as well.

Instruction in arithmetic suffers most seriously from the failure to teach the child that certain rules apply to a variety of problems. For example, the child is taught that whenever distance problems are posed he should apply the rule "$d = rt$," and he does this automatically once he learns the rule. But if he is faced with a problem about water flow through a pipe (which also has rate and time variables), he will not know what to do unless he is taught specifically that the total volume of water flowing through a pipe equals the rate of flow times its duration. If the child were first taught that rate and time are general characteristics of many phenomena in nature, he would be more likely to generate the correct hypothesis for any problem involving rate and time concepts. The suggestion here is for teaching *multiple* applications of basic concepts and rules so that the child will not rigidly associate these rules with specific kinds of problems.

The Problem with Miniaturization. These comments about current educational practice are related to a more general criticism of the tendency of schools to promote a *specialized, miniaturized view of knowledge.* Most teachers and parents agree that one of the goals of education is to enable the child to gain maximal efficiency and ease with technical skills that he will need in a future vocation. The physicist will have to understand atomic theory; the accountant, mathematics; the doctor, physiology. Most of these necessary technical skills are learned during the college and professional years, when they are taught in the forms in which they will be used. However, there is an unquestioned assumption in educational practice that the earlier such material is presented, the easier it will be for the student to master it during late adolescence and early adulthood. Stated most simply, the argument is that one "babies up" to understanding a subject. As a result, miniaturized versions of geometry, geography, and science are given to children in grades one through four.

The value of such procedures is apt to be minimal. We do not give the child a miniaturized model for social skills. We want young boys to grow up to be good husbands, but we do not believe that a seven-year-old should play "husband" with his mother in preparation for becoming a good spouse fifteen years later. We assume that exposure to parental affection will prepare him for the marriage role. Our theory of how a child's personality develops guides our actions. Since we do not have an adequate theory for the development of academic talents, we miniaturize high school and college material. We might begin to develop better strategies if we cast off age-old dogma like miniaturization and analyzed curriculum content.

Consider the subject of geometry. One of the major skills required in geometry is the ability to visualize in three dimensions. Thus it would seem wise to give the seven-year-old practice in visualization, rather than having him draw graphs with rules and compasses. Experiences in visualization might include locating objects with the eyes closed, tracing letters and words by walking with the eyes closed, and practice in imagining and constructing three-dimensional maps, designs, and models of buildings.

Similarly, training in social studies can be better provided by having students compile and interpret familiar events, rather than by giving them a *Reader's Digest* version of the discovery of America. For the essence of history is interpretation of objective descriptions of the past. An exciting fifth-grade assignment would be to ask the students to write down everything that happened the day before in the classroom. A comparison of the students' descriptions would reveal the distortions of the events in each child's mind. The teacher might even try to structure class discussion so that the students could see the reasons for their different perceptions—for example, by pointing out how their location in the classroom might have influenced what they saw or heard or how their attitudes toward certain events colored their interpretations.

There will, of course, be a small body of emotionally neutral fact that most students will agree upon. A discussion of these areas of accord would provide the class with an important insight into the nature of historical writing. The teacher might then initiate a unit on the Revolutionary War and have the class compare the histories of that period written by British and American writers. The reasons for the differences in facts emphasized and in interpretations imposed would generate an exciting discussion.

Since there has been an increase in politically slanted newspapers, the teacher might also compare so-called objective descriptions of events by several papers. The class should analyze the omissions, exaggerations, and varied interpretations of the same event. Finally, the teacher should continually emphasize how the historian's interpretation goes beyond the facts and how his biases affect both his interpretations and his original collection of information.

High school history and science teachers might join forces to help the student appreciate the similarities and differences in these two disciplines. For example, both the historian and the scientist are faced with the task of selecting facts to interpret. But the scientist has more exact ways to check the objectivity of his information and the validity of his inferences. This discussion might be followed by a unit on the nature of truth: "How does a man know what to believe?" The teacher might select the experience of pain as a theme and ask the class to consider how different types of men might try to understand that phenomenon. The natural scientist, wedded to the empirical method of gaining knowledge, observes people in states of pain and measures their sweating, heartbeat, or brain waves. The philosopher constructs a logical argument on how man thinks about pain, his reactions to it, and how social institutions help him to avoid this unpleasant state. The artist or poet constructs a personal conception. Each view is partially true, for each speaks to a different aspect of the experience. The student must be shown that a complex idea is never totally known, that truth must be pursued in varied ways. If he realizes that each insight into an idea or event is only part of the whole, he will be more appreciative of man's slow progress toward wisdom.

The miniaturization approach to knowledge is also apparent in the science programs of elementary schools, which typically expose the child to bees, rabbits, and ants. The assumption seems to be that early exposure to animals studied in the laboratory leads to greater skill or interest in science. It probably does not. The essence of science is explanation, not observation, and explanation involves making up reasonable interpretations for strange events. Practice in explanation is far better preparation for science than caring for six hamsters.

There are many ways to give the student practice in scientific explanation. For example, the teacher might put iodine on a wet piece of white bread, call the students' attention to the dramatic blue color, and ask them to guess what might have caused the event. A third-grade class might come close to inventing molecular theory. Or the teacher might ask the class to guess why the sound of thunder is heard after lightning is seen. On a day in which a thunderstorm occurs during the period, the students might even be able to estimate the speed of sound if they are led carefully by the teacher. There are many other familiar events that puzzle young children—why boys run faster than girls, why eyes are of different colors, what keeps planes up in the air, why wet clothes dry on a clothesline, what causes the bubbles in boiling water, how a magnet works, and why it is possible to die from a bad cold.

The presentation of an everyday problem of interest that the child has not yet solved will provoke him to generate possible solutions. Each suggested solution should be checked for logic and for consistency with facts that the class believes to be true. The teacher should keep a record of class solutions for several months and should then point out to the students the basic similarities in all their answers. Their solutions to why bread turns blue in iodine, why leaves turn yellow in October, and why lobsters become pink in boiling water rest on similar ideas.

These suggestions are intended to alert the teacher to the value of thinking through the rationale of the subject she is teaching and of analyzing the mental structures and processes needed for competence in that subject. Once this analysis is done, the teacher will become aware of potential soft spots in class presentations and will be able to build up a reservoir of examples for dealing with different problems.

Programmed Instruction and Teaching Machines. The limitations of the miniaturization approach to knowledge have been a major component in many curriculum reforms. One of the most important of these reforms is the use of programmed instruction and teaching machines. The teaching machine is defined as "a carefully prepared program for a specific segment of knowledge housed in some apparatus that presents the programmed material and indicates to the student when a response is right and when it is wrong." Unlike most educational innovations, the teaching machine is based on a theory of how children learn. In addition, the machines are more readily available than good teachers. Thus many parents and educators believe that proper use of a sufficient number of teaching machines will solve the awesome problems of contemporary education. The machine clearly has a useful role, but it is not a panacea.

There are three basic psychological assumptions behind the use of teaching machines, each of which requires examination. First, the use of the teaching machine is based on the notion that responses are learned more effectively if there is minimal delay between the child's offering of an answer and his subsequent knowledge of its accuracy. However, some recent experiments and reflection on the psychological nature of children lead us to question the universal application of this principle. The notion that learning is impeded by a long delay between the making of a response and delivery of a reward is based on results from learning experiments with animals. If a hungry rat presses a bar or runs a complex maze for food, and the food appears thirty seconds after the action rather than immediately, the animal is not likely to learn how to press the bar or run the maze. Thus many people assume that if a child makes a response and does not get the correct answer quickly (the answer is his reward), he will be unlikely to learn anything. But such a conclusion neglects the fact that human beings are thinking creatures who brood about what they are doing as well as what they have done. Since people can and do fill the time between making a response and receiving the correct answer by thinking about their behavior, the importance of an immediate answer is minimized.

In one study, a group of undergraduate students was given a multiple-choice test and informed of the answer to each question immediately; another group of students received each answer after a ten-second delay. All the students were then given a retention test to measure what they had learned and were tested again five days later. There were no differences in score on the first retention test between those who received each answer immediately and those who were told the answer after ten seconds. However, on the test given five days later, the students who received delayed answers performed much better than those who received immediate answers. (Sassen-rath and Yonge, 1969.) It is likely that the students were mentally rehearsing each problem and answer during the ten-second delay, and this extra time for synthesis and rehearsal aided their learning.

Another study tested students on their knowledge of statistics. One group of students received their test scores immediately—as the tests were turned in; each student was then instructed to find the correct responses to his mistakes. A second group learned their test scores twenty-four hours later. When the test was administered again a week later, the students who had had to wait twenty-four hours to learn of their performance on the first test obtained higher scores than those who had been informed immediately. (Daniel, 1968.)

Since some students brood about their performance on tests, delay of an answer can on occasion facilitate learning. Suppose a child is being taught to associate a color word with an animal word. The teacher says "bird," and if the child responds with a color word, the teacher says "good." If the child does not say a color word, the teacher says nothing. If the teacher imposed a delay before saying the reward "good" after the child stated a color word, the child would have time to consider the two words and the relation necessary to solve the problem. In order for material in short-term memory to be transferred to long-term memory, there must be time for this synthesis, time for the implicit rehearsal of information. Since imposing a delay in the delivery of an answer gives the child a chance to rehearse and synthesize information, it can have a beneficial effect on learning. Thus the first principle guiding the use of teaching machines *is not true all the time.*

A second assumption behind the use of the teaching machine is that the systematic structuring of a large unit of knowledge is superior to a random presentation of that knowledge. To some extent, this principle is true, for a teacher's lecture on a topic cannot possibly simulate the orderliness of a carefully thought-out program. But as with the principle of delay, there are exceptions. For example, students majoring in education were given two programmed-instruction units while sitting at a typewriter terminal linked to a computer system. One group of students was assigned programs that were ordered and logical; another group was assigned programs that were completely disorganized. The two units to be learned consisted of a modern mathematics program on the transformation of numbers in the base-10 system to equivalent values in a nondecimal system and a program on the anatomy of the ear. The unit on numbers lent itself to organization and was therefore expected to benefit from logical programming. The unit on the anatomy of the ear consisted of a set of unrelated anatomical facts to be memorized and was assumed to derive relatively little benefit from a structured program.

As expected, there were no differences in ease of learning for test performance on the anatomy unit between the group of students given the structured material and the group given the disorganized program. It did not make any difference for rote memory whether the units were programmed or not. However, on the mathematics unit the students with the logical program made *more errors* than the group with the disordered program. The first group of students made more errors as the ordered program progressed because the material became more difficult. The group given the disorganized program made significantly more errors than the first group during the early stages of the unit, but by the last part of the program they became more confident and made fewer errors. The scrambled program was also better for bright students than for average students, for it was more challenging than the ordered program and led to greater student involvement. (Wodtke *et al.*, 1968.)

Thus, assuming a student is motivated, he is more likely to learn when he tries to impose a structure on new material than when the structure is given to him ready-made. The careful structuring of information ignores the effect of increased problem difficulty on expectancy of failure and the motivational value of challenge. Programs make new material maximally easy to understand, on the assumption that the student *wants* to learn the material as easily as possible. Some children do not want the task made too easy; they thrive on challenge. The fun is in getting to the top of the mountain, not in being there. As a result, some children find programmed materials boring, or even condescending, and they do poorer than if the material had been presented in a less systematic manner. Thus the second principle guiding the use of teaching machines *has occasional limitations, especially for brighter students.*

The third assumption behind the use of the teaching machine is that the child learns best when adults stay out of his way, when he is able to have a solitary dialogue with the material to be learned. In the discussion of motives in the first part of this book it was suggested that just the opposite is true, for the young child is often more highly motivated to learn when he feels he will obtain the responses of a teacher.

In one experiment on this issue, a group of fourth-grade students worked with a teacher on a programmed sequence on the geography of Japan. A second group of pupils worked with a teacher aide and the materials. A third group worked alone with the program, and a fourth group was given no instruction at all. The students exposed to the teacher with the program performed much better than those exposed to the program alone. The assumption that adults should not be involved in the child's learning is clearly not supported by this experiment. (Ryan, 1968.)

In another study, a group of high school boys worked alone on a programmed unit on number concepts, recording their answers in a booklet. A second group watched the teacher and other students interact with the program in the fashion of traditional recitation. The teacher wrote each problem on the blackboard and the students came forward to recite. A third group was made up of those students from the second group who answered the teacher's questions aloud. A fourth group watched and listened while the teacher recited each question of the program to herself and then answered it herself, as if she were describing her own thoughts. A fifth group was given no training at all. In a test given to all students at the end of the experiment, the first four groups performed better than the fifth group. But none of the four experimental groups performed better than any other. Watching the teacher was as effective as doing the program alone. (Craig, 1968.) Thus the third assumption behind the use of teaching machines also *has its exceptions*.

We must conclude therefore that the three basic principles behind the use of the teaching machine—delay of reward, structured programming, and elimination of the adult—are not always true. When these principles do not hold, the failure can usually be explained by taking into account the motives and expectancies of the child. The child's view of the machine is a critical factor in the success of any program. What does the act of sitting at a machine represent to him? His view will depend on whether he believes that completion of seven units by Friday afternoon will bring the teacher's praise and recognition, avoidance of punishment, or internal satisfaction. The child's feeling of freedom to use the machine is also critical. Does he have a choice of using a machine or a textbook, or must he use one or the other? The machine will be viewed more positively by the child who feels that he has a choice.

As in most issues, there is no absolute statement than can be made about the value of teaching machines. The machine has gained popularity because it enables educators to do something effective at a time when it is not clear what should be done. Action always reduces apprehension in a time of crisis, and it is easier to change the material than to alter the child's behavior or his relationship to the teacher. But in the long run it may be more advantageous to improve the child's motivation to learn. The teaching machine should neither be rejected out of hand nor be embraced as a cure to the problem of pupil apathy. The machine's novelty should be exploited fully; its emphasis on rational analysis of a segment of knowledge should be heeded. But inflexible reliance on the machine for all children and for all types of learning is probably unwise.

Curriculum Changes. The concern with programmed materials is only one part of a general effort to facilitate learning by improving school curriculum. If the teacher is dissatisfied with a child's progress in school, she can alter either the child's behavior, her own behavior, or the curriculum. If a school decides to devote effort to curriculum, it is natural for teachers and administrators to exaggerate the importance of curricula. A unit of any subject matter must have two characteristics to be successful: it must attract and maintain the attention of pupil *and* teacher, and it must be paced in a way that is comprehensible to the child. The curriculum reforms of the last ten years have generally shown an awareness of these goals, for they have attempted to increase the interest value of the material while organizing the information into a paced set of exercises.

Although it is generally assumed that a curriculum change is made in order to increase the child's interest, the change often has its most beneficial effect on the teacher. Once a curriculum change is instituted, the teacher can no longer use well-practiced, stereotyped approaches. As a result, she becomes more emotionally involved in her instruction, for she feels she is testing herself with the new material. This challenge acts as a tonic and increases her enthusiasm in the classroom. A change in curriculum does as much for the teacher as it does for the child, for the novelty brought to the classroom by the change will recruit involvement from both participants.

There is no ideal or perfect curriculum. In order to attract and maintain the interest of child and teacher any program must be changed periodically. This conclusion, which seems pessimistic on the surface, should not cool the earnest enthusiasm and inventiveness of those who try to improve the quality of teaching materials. An awareness of the role of novelty and surprise will benefit any curriculum effort.

Teachers typically set up routine schedules that are repeated year after year. This strategy probably arose in part from the belief that the young child needs certainty in his life. He is insecure and anxious if he does not know what is going to happen next. This apprehension about the future is true for the young child in the opening years of school, when many procedures are novel and the child is vigilant and occasionally confused. But by the time he is in grade four, he appears to become bored with school activities and resistant to the requests of the teacher. Some critics of the school have argued that this apathy is the child's way of telling the teacher that he has mastered the uncertainty of being in school and is ready for some novel routines to "figure out." Children are more concerned with coping with their environment than with mastering academic skills. The introduction of new routines for the child to "figure out" may revive some of the enthusiasm seen in earlier grades. Fourth and fifth grades are good times to institute changes in routine. These changes can take the form of regular use of movies and tape recorders, discussions led by pupils, team-teaching, and even the bold announcement of surprise events that the young student cannot anticipate—the school's version of a sneak preview.

EVALUATION

The fourth step in the problem-solving process is the evaluation of possible solutions. There are significant differences in the degree to which children evaluate the validity of their cognitive processes. Some children pause to evaluate the quality of their thinking and the accuracy of their conclusions. They mentally analyze their ideas and censor many possible solutions before they ever report or act upon them. These children are called *reflective*. Other children, of equal intelligence, accept and report the first idea they think of and often act upon that idea with minimal consideration of its appropriateness or quality. These children are called *impulsive*.

The evaluation process influences the entire domain of thought, including the accuracy of initial perceptions, the accuracy of recall in memory, and the quality of reasoning. It appears that the tendency to be reflective or impulsive can be previewed as early as two years of age, which indicates that this psychological tendency is moderately stable over time.

Measuring Evaluation. A good index of the child's tendency to be reflective or impulsive in evaluating his ideas is the Matching Familiar Figures Test (see Figure 3), in which the child is asked

FIGURE 3 Sample item from the Matching Familiar Figures Test.

127

to select one picture in a set of six variations that is identical with a picture called the standard. Thus in Figure 3 the child would be asked to pick the tree in the two rows of three that is exactly like the tree that sits alone as the standard. The examiner records the time the child takes to offer his first answer as well as the number of errors he makes. The faster the child makes his decision as to which picture is correct, the more mistakes he is likely to make. In general, as the child gets older he takes longer to offer his first answer and hence makes fewer errors. Children who display reflective behavior on this particular test tend to be reflective in a variety of other situations. They wait longer in answering a question, make fewer errors in reading textual material, and are less likely to make incorrect guesses on reading tests.

Fortunately it is possible to make an impulsive child more reflective and an overly reflective child a little more impulsive. The teacher's own evaluative behavior can be an important factor. A reflective teacher tends to make the children in her class more reflective, whereas an impulsive teacher tends to produce impulsivity in class. In one experiment, first-grade teachers were classified as being reflective or impulsive. Children from each teacher's classroom were then tested for reflective or impulsive behavior in September and again the following May to see if daily encounter with the teacher influenced their attitudes. All the children tended to change in a direction that matched the tempo of their teacher. The change was most dramatic for impulsive boys who had reflective teachers with a great deal of experience. These boys showed a significant change toward a reflective attitude. (Yondo and Kagan, 1968.)

Bases for Reflective and Impulsive Behavior. The major cause of a reflective attitude is anxiety over making a mistake. The greater the child's fear of error, the more likely he is to be reflective. The reflective child wishes to be correct and therefore tries to avoid mistakes at any cost. For reasons not yet understood, the impulsive child does not seem to be particularly upset about mistakes and therefore responds quickly. Several studies have shown that American schoolchildren become more reflective with age than children of other cultures. The American value system encourages children to avoid error, to avoid the humiliation of being wrong; thus young children become excessively inhibited and cautious.

As suggested several times, the teacher should alleviate excessive anxiety in the young child. She should encourage the reflective child to guess when he is not sure and to be less critical of his mistakes. She should encourage the impulsive child to slow down, to think about the accuracy and quality of his answers, and to be concerned with the possibility of error. Thus the teacher must adopt diametrically different tactics with these two groups of children. She might use tests like the Matching Familiar Figures Test to diagnose reflective and impulsive children if she cannot do so from observing their behavior in the classroom.

The need to adopt different tactics for reflective and impulsive children is a good example of why the teacher cannot use one curriculum or one set of teaching strategies with all children. Children differ not only in their tendency to be reflective or impulsive but in their vocabulary, concepts, and rules; in their hostility or affection for the teacher; and in their view of the sex-role appropriateness of schoolwork. The optimal school experience is one that is tailored to these differences.

IMPLEMENTATION

The final step in the problem-solving process is implementation, or the deduction of a conclusion from an idea that has been generated. It should be obvious that the generation of an idea and the deduction of a conclusion are intimately related processes, for to realize that both coral and butterflies are living things is simultaneously to deduce that each grows and will eventually die. Moreover, these two cognitive processes are typically regarded as the essence of thinking. Deduction is the application of a rule—formal or informal—to solve a problem. Hence of the many sets of mental structures that control the quality of deduction the most important is the child's storehouse of rules, which typically increases with age. Some of the child's rules are formal, like the mathematical rule "$8^2 = 64$." Others are informal, like the rule "Thundershowers occur in summer." Possession of these rules is critical to the successful solution of problems.

One of the important theoretical questions in psychology centers on whether there are basic changes in the child's understanding and use of rules as he matures from the preschool years through adolescence. As indicated earlier, some psychologists assume that the child merely learns more rules each day, storing them for future use, and that no rule is necessarily too difficult for a child of any age to comprehend and apply appropriately. Other psychologists believe that some rules are inherently too difficult for young children to understand and that there are maturational stages in the development of thought. This is the thesis of Jean Piaget, which is considered in detail in the following section because of its importance to educational practice.

Intellectual Development

PIAGET'S THEORY OF INTELLECTUAL GROWTH

Jean Piaget is probably the most important student of intellectual development of this century. His views about thought and intelligence are complex and provocative and have major implications for education. For Piaget the word "intelligence" has a very specific definition. Intelligence is "the coordination of operations." An operation resembles a rule, but it is not identical with it. An operation is a special kind of mental routine, and one of its major characteristics is that it is reversible—that is, it has a logical opposite. For example, we can square the number 8 to get 64 or perform the reverse operation and extract the square root of 64. We can break a six-ounce, circular piece of clay into two elliptical pieces or perform the reverse operation and combine the two pieces of clay into the same circular shape again. In each of these examples a reversible operation is performed in which nothing is lost; we can return mentally to where we began. The gradual acquisition of these special kinds of rules is, according to Piaget, the heart of intellectual growth.

Not all the statements that we have called rules are operations, according to Piaget's definition. For example, the five-year-old has learned the rule that if he dirties his shirt his mother will become angry with him. But this rule is not reversible, for there is no routine that will restore the mother's good mood. The child does not have a rule that will enable him to recreate that prior state. Similarly, most of the everyday rules that we use to guide our lives—"Water comes from faucets," "Fire can burn paper," "Cars cause pollution"—are not reversible and are therefore not operations.

Piaget believes that the child passes through stages on his way to achieving the end state called adult Western thought and suggests that a child gradually comes to arrive at this goal by passing through four major stages of intellectual growth: the sensorimotor stage (birth to eighteen months of age), the preoperational stage (eighteen months to age seven), the stage of concrete operations (age seven to twelve), and the stage of formal operations (age twelve onward).

The Sensorimotor Stage. The sensorimotor stage comprises the period in the infant's life prior to the acquisition of language when his intelligence is seen in his actions. When a one-year-old wants a rattle resting on a pillow a few feet away from him, he pulls the pillow toward him. The child uses the pillow to attain his goal. This behavior is not an operation but a scheme of action. The pulling of an object is a general response that the infant uses to solve a variety of similar problems. The kicking of the side of a crib in order to make a mobile move is another example of a scheme of action. The infant possesses many such schemes. He can kick, shake, hit, bang, and sock, and when a new event is presented to him he may display any one of these schemes. The child's mouthing of a toy he has never seen before is an example of Piaget's concept of assimilation, which is one of the two basic ideas in his theory.

Assimilation is the process by which the child uses an existing scheme of action or operation to deal with a new object or stimulus. At any given time the infant has a set of sensorimotor schemes; the older child has a set of operations. New objects and new ideas are assimilated to old, existing schemes. The act of recognizing an ultramodern chair as an object that one sits on is a good illustration of the concept of assimilation.

Opposed to assimilation is the process of *accommodation,* in which the child makes a mental adjustment to a new object or idea. The child changes a scheme of action or an operation in order to understand a new experience. The two-year-old who has never seen a small bar magnet is likely to assimilate it to an existing scheme for small objects and hence bang it, suck it, or use it to make a noise. But if he accidentally discovers the unique characteristic of the magnet—namely, that it attracts metal—he immediately accommodates to it. He will develop a new scheme of action and will now apply the magnet to pieces of metal and watch the effect. Hence the process of accommodation changes his whole understanding of magnets. This example captures the essence of Piaget's view of mental growth. The development of intelligence is a continual process in which the tension between assimilation and accommodation is being resolved. The child is always in conflict, torn between the urge to use old ideas for new problems and the need to change old rules and concepts in order to solve new problems more effectively. Piaget believes that intellectual growth occurs when old schemes are altered in order to provide a better adaptation to a new situation.

The Preoperational Stage. In the preoperational stage the young child acquires knowledge of symbols and concepts, many of them in the form of language. These new cognitive units begin to dominate his mental life. Now the child treats a piece of clay as if it were a cookie and feeds it to a doll, or he treats a block of wood as if it were an automobile and moves it around, making a noise as he travels. This tendency to treat objects as if they were symbolic of something else is an essential characteristic of the preoperational stage of development. Piaget offers an illustration in which a doll is treated as if it were a live baby:

> At 2 years 1 month, J put her doll's head through the balcony railing with its face turned toward the street and began to tell it what she saw, "You see the lake and trees, you see a carriage or house." The same day she seated her doll on a sofa and told it what she herself had seen in the garden. (Piaget, *Play, Dreams, and Imitation,* p. 127.)

Although the child of three or four is capable of symbolic behavior, he is not yet capable of operational thinking. His language and concepts are not organized into operations. That significant event occurs sometime after five or six years of age, during the stage of concrete operations.

The Stage of Concrete Operations. In the stage of concrete operations the child acquires four important cognitive processes.

Briefly, they involve the ability to represent sequences of events (mental representation) and the realizations that objects do not change their essential weight or volume merely because their shape is changed (conservation), that parts and wholes are logically related (class inclusion), and finally that objects can be arranged according to some quantifiable dimension (serialization).

Mental representation. The child who is in the stage of concrete operations can represent an entire sequence of actions relevant to some goal. For example, he is able to draw all the various turns he makes in going to school and has an overall picture of that route. Thus if one of the streets were blocked he might be able to find another way to the goal. The child who is in the stage of concrete operations is able to represent the steps to a goal and the goal itself in one united structure.

Conservation. The child under five or six years of age believes that if a liquid or a solid is changed in shape, its volume or mass must also change. In contrast, the child who has reached the stage of concrete operations knows that a piece of clay or a glass of milk can be made into a different shape or put into a different container without changing the amount of substance involved. In one of Piaget's most famous experiments, a five-year-old is shown two balls of plasticine of equal mass and of the same shape. The child is asked whether the two balls have the same amount of plasticine and typically nods affirmatively. The examiner then either flattens one of the balls of plasticine so that it resembles a dish or rolls the ball into a thin, snakelike pattern. He then asks the child which one has the greater amount, or whether there is the same amount in both objects. The child of four or five will regard the two forms as unequal in quantity. He may say that the snakelike pattern has more plasticine because it is longer. Two years later, however, he will insist that both the original ball and the snake have the same amount, because "although the snake is longer, it is thinner." Better yet, the child may say that he can make the snakelike pattern back into the ball again merely be reshaping it. These responses indicate that the child is aware of the compensatory dimensions of length and width.

The child who is in the stage of concrete operations also realizes that the *number* of objects in an array is conserved, regardless of changes in the shape or arrangement of the objects. For example, if two rows of six pennies each are placed one above the other so that the rows are of equal length, both the five-year-old and the seven-year-old will acknowledge that the rows have the same number of pennies. However, if one row of pennies is placed closer together, the younger child will say that the longer row has more pennies—that is, his concept of more is linked to the perceptual aspect of the row and not to the idea of number. The child who is in the stage of concrete operations will insist that both rows have the same number of pennies.

Class inclusion. The child who is in the stage of concrete operations has acquired the ability to reason simultaneously about the whole and part of the whole. If a five-year-old is shown eight orange buttons and four yellow buttons and asked, "Are there more orange buttons or more buttons?" he is likely to say, "There are more orange buttons." The seven-year-old, in contrast, will insist that there are more buttons, realizing that "buttons" is a category including both the orange and the yellow.

Serialization. Finally, the child who is in the stage of concrete operations is able to arrange objects according to some quantifiable dimension, such as length, width, or weight. In contrast, the child of four or five cannot arrange balls of different diameters according to their size. In should be apparent that the child who has not mastered the operation of serialization will have difficulty learning about arithmetic and the quantifiable dimension of numbers.

In summary, the child of seven or eight who is in the stage of concrete operations has acquired an important set of cognitive rules. He believes firmly that length, mass, weight, and number remain the same despite superficial modifications in the shape or arrangement of objects. He can reason about the whole and its parts and is able to order objects according to quantifiable dimensions. These four cognitive rules are critical for much of school learning, and this is perhaps one reason that school entrance is postponed until the child is six or seven years of age.

The Stage of Formal Operations. In the stage of formal operational thinking the child displays three new qualities. First, his analysis of a problem is systematic. He considers all the possible solutions to a particular problem. For example, if he is trying to determine the shortest route from school to a baseball field across town, he will review mentally all the possible routes and will know when he has considered all the possibilities, including the shortest route. Consider the following puzzle: "A man came home after a two-week vacation and found all the windows on one side of his house broken. What could have happened?" The young child usually responds to such a problem by stating the first reason that satisfies him; thus he might say, "Some boys threw rocks at the windows." The adolescent is more likely to generate several reasons for the disaster—an attack, a rockslide, a hailstorm, an internal gas explosion. The ability and willingness to examine all the possible solutions is an important characteristic of the child in the stage of formal operations.

Second, the adolescent's thought in the stage of formal operations is self-consciously logical, resembling that of the scientist. The adolescent is capable of thinking about ideas and propositions that may violate reality and be completely fanciful. Consider the following syllogistic problem: "If all cows with purple udders have yellow calves, is it true that a yellow calf must have had a mother with purple udders?" The seven-year-old will object to this problem immediately by insisting that there are no yellow calves and no cows with purple udders. The adolescent, in contrast, is not bothered by the fact that the problem is unrelated to reality and is capable of accepting the propositions, reasoning about the problem, and concluding that the hypothesis is not tenable.

Finally, the adolescent who is in the stage of formal operations organizes his operations into more complicated, higher-order structures that enable him to solve major classes of problems. Consider the problem "What number is four times its square?" The nine-year-old is likely to begin this problem by trial and error, testing first one number and then another by the operations of addition and multiplication, and is unlikely to arrive at the correct answer. The adolescent, in contrast, has learned a higher-order operation—namely, the setting up of an algebraic equation—and he quickly sets the equation $4x = x^2$ and finds the answer to be 4. The adolescent has learned to combine the separate operations of division and multiplication into the more complex operation of an algebraic equation. This more complex unit is called a *combinative structure*.

In essence, the thought process that occurs during the period of formal operations is characterized by the tendency to isolate the elements of the problem, to systematically explore all the possible solutions regardless of their hypothetical quality, and to reflect upon the consistency of rules. This last point is of great interest to psychologists and is related to the general observation that adolescents are broody and introspective. The fifteen-year-old continually reflects upon the rules he possesses, questioning their accuracy and fidelity. He is self-conscious about his own thoughts and about what he knows. It is not an accident that the child first becomes introspective during adolescence. The adolescent thinks about himself, his role in life, his plans, and the integrity of his values. Many adolescents are concerned with the validity of their beliefs and the beliefs of their parents. This self-examination is not seen in preadolescent children. The adolescent, unlike the child of eight or nine, is concerned with the hypothetical, the future, the remote, and the ideal. As one adolescent remarked, "I found myself thinking about my future, and then I began to think about why I was thinking about my future, and then I began to think about why I was thinking about why I was thinking about my future." This concern with the validity of thought is characteristic of the stage of formal operations.

Evaluation of Piaget. Piaget's suggestions about the acquisition of the operations of conservation, class inclusion, and serialization seem generally true for Western children. But these concepts are most relevant to mathematics and physics and are less obviously important for biological and social phenomena. The strict relation between a whole and its parts that holds in mathematics has limited application to living cells or to the behavior of people. The concept of a nation is more than the sum of the number of people in it or the number of its territorial divisions. Moreover, the child knows that death, unlike the quantity of water, is not conserved; there is no reversible operation we can call upon to restore life. Piaget's observations of certain sequences in intellectual development are essentially correct. But it is still not clear how *general* these principles are and whether the emphasis on operations as the essence of intellectual functioning is the most frutiful way to describe the enigma of thought.

INTELLIGENCE

Human beings like to rank people and things into the categories of good, better, and best. We are not satisfied with noting that a rose is a deep red; we feel pressed to add that it is the loveliest flower in the garden. As noted earlier, man automatically gives a good-bad score to most of his experiences. He also performs this evaluation on himself, for he views homeliness as bad and attractiveness as good; weakness as bad and strength as good. Of the many attributes of man, three typically receive special attention in all cultures: physical qualities, inner feelings, and skills. There are very few cultures that do not have special words to describe how a person looks, how he feels, and how competent he is—and these words imply that certain appearances, feelings, and skills are good while others are bad.

But each culture's system of values is somewhat arbitrary and may not be valid for another group or for its own people at another time in history. Standards of physical appearance have always varied with time and place. In seventeenth-century Europe women whom we would regard as overweight and unattractive were viewed as beautiful. A comparison of a Rubens nude with that of a Gauguin reveals this changing standard of attractiveness.

Evaluations of inner feeling states also shift with time and location. Some cultures celebrate the emotional feeling of being possessed by a metaphysical force. Modern Western society, with its rational bias, has denigrated that mystical experience and, since Freud, has promoted the belief that absence of fear is the significant emotional state to attain. We use the word "neurotic" to describe those who are unable to hold on to this precious state. However, in the average citizen's mind the evaluative word "neurotic" has come to be associated with any undesirable feeling, regardless of its specific quality or origin. Thus many members of our society now apply "neurotic" to those who take drugs, because they believe that the emotional state produced by drugs is a bad one.

The human skills that are tagged as good or bad also vary with time and social group. Every society sets up certain talents as most desirable and gives those who possess these talents a label. Americans use the word "intelligent" to describe those people who possess the skills that the society regards as important. Among African Bushmen, those who possess exceptional skill at hunting and tracking are given a designation that has the same connotation as our word "intelligent."

In the late nineteenth century Sir Francis Galton suggested that people with extremely sensitive vision and hearing were intelligent because the dominant brain theory of the day emphasized the importance of transmission of outside sensory information to the central nervous system. Today we associate skill in language and reasoning with intelligence because our theories of the brain have changed. But we still use the word "intelligent" to designate those people who have more of the skills that we happen to believe are "better."

From a scientific point of view, it is clear that words like "neurotic" and "intelligent" are of little theoretical use, for they are primarily evaluative and explain very little. But most members of our society—scientists as well as nonscientists—believe, first, that some people's brains are better organized than others' and, second, that this difference should reflect itself in different psychological talents and actions. Thus we feel pressed to designate certain attributes as intelligent, despite the fact that there will be changes in the skills so designated as a function of scientific theory and cultural biases. Since psychological theory is presently immature, it gives little direction to those who search for the meaning of intelligence. But it is unlikely that our culture will tear out the dictionary entry for that word and promise not to use it any more. Hence it should be useful to consider the various meanings that intelligence has in our society at this particular time.

Intelligence as Adaptation to the Environment. The ability of an organism to adapt to the specific environmental niche in which it lives and grows is, for the biologist, the most important attribute of an animal species. Successful adaptation depends on the ability to resist predators, to reproduce the next generation, and to cope with new environmental pressures by learning new habits and through anatomical and physiological changes. Evolutionary studies have shown that some species, like the opossum, have survived for many thousands of generations, whereas other species, like the lovely heron, are about to become extinct. If intelligence is defined as the ability to adapt to an ecological niche, then the opossum must be more intelligent than the heron. Since this conclusion contradicts our intuitions, the view of intelligence as successful adaptation has never become popular. But this attitude is a matter of taste, not logic.

To a certain extent, Piaget's theory of intelligence as the coordination of mental operations promotes the biological prejudice described above. As noted earlier, Piaget believes the growth of intelligence to be the resolution of the tension between assimilation and accommodation, between using old ideas for new problems and changing old ideas to solve new problems. Intellectual growth is adaptation to the new through alteration of old strategies, and the intelligent child is one who possesses the operations that enable him to solve new problems.

Intelligence as the Ability to Learn New Skills. Most people regard intelligence as the ability to learn new ideas and skills. One version of this view assumes that the more intelligent a child is, the faster he will be able to learn *any* new idea or skill. This belief rests on the notion that there is a generalized intelligence capable of acquiring new competences regardless of their specific nature. Opposed to this view is the belief that learning is governed by a set of specific intelligences, and that the ability to learn new skills depends on the specific skill involved. Thus the man who learns a foreign language quickly may not have such an easy time learning to sail.

The question of a generalized intelligence versus a set of specific intelligences has been the subject of much controversy among psychologists and is reflected in our ambivalent attitude toward experts. We show preference for the doctrine of specific intelligences in our belief that the President of the United States should be surrounded by counselors of different expertise—economists, social scientists, physicists, and so on. Similarly, as individuals, we tend to seek advice from varied people according to the problem. We ask for help with our fears from a psychiatrist, help with our investments from a broker, and advice on building a house from an architect. However, our society also supports the idea of a generalized intelligence, for we are willing to listen to the advice of a Nobel laureate in physics on how to solve the racial crises in our schools, on the assumption that brilliance in one area indicates equally profound understanding of problems far removed from the domain of demonstrated ability.

It is this issue that lies at the center of the intense controversy surrounding the meaning of intelligence and the value of the IQ score. Parents and teachers who believe that intelligence reflects the ability to learn new skills with ease are often impressed with the intelligence test because a ten-year-old's IQ score does predict to some degree his grades in high school and college. But is this possible because there is a general ability to learn that is stable over time and place or because the skills that are taught in most high schools and colleges are intimately related to the skills measured on the intelligence test? The ability of the IQ test to predict high school English grades may merely reflect a specific intelligence—in this case, the ability to master English concepts and vocabulary.

The IQ Test as a Measure of Intelligence. It is an unfortunate fact that many Americans hold the belief that the IQ score defines intelligence. As parents they are anxious about how high or low their child's IQ is and often attach too much value to this particular characteristic. Most Americans believe that a child's inheritance is the major determinant of his IQ score, that his IQ is not likely to change over the course of his lifetime, and that IQ can be measured at any point in life, including early infancy. Each of these beliefs is a serious exaggeration of the facts and indeed approaches a mistruth. Many people do not realize that the majority of questions on intelligence tests do not measure the child's ability to learn anything new; rather, they ask him only whether he knows a particular fact or piece of knowledge. Yet most people regard intelligence as the ability to learn a new idea or skill. Hence the IQ test fails to measure the essential characteristic of most people's definition of intelligence.

The IQ test is, however, an excellent measure of how much the child has learned about the dominant symbols, concepts, and rules in his culture, and this is why it predicts school grades as well as it does. More specifically, the IQ score is an efficient way to summarize the degree to which a child has learned the vocabulary, beliefs, and rules of *middle-class* American society. We know that middle-class children are more consistently encouraged than lower-class children to learn to read, spell, add, and write and to acquire the concepts that are measured on IQ tests. Thus the child's IQ score, his social class, and his school grades are all positively related to one another. The IQ test is extremely useful because it can predict how easily a child of eight will master the elements of calculus or history when he enters college. However, the specific questions asked on intelligence tests have been deliberately chosen to make this prediction possible. The child is asked to define the word "shilling" rather than the word "rap"; he is asked to state the similarity between a "fly" and a "tree" rather than the similarity between "fuzz" and "Uncle Tom"; he is asked to copy a geometric design rather than to climb a pole; he is asked what he should do "if he lost one of his friend's toys" rather than what he should do "if he were attacked by three bullies."

The IQ test should not be rejected, however, merely because it is biased toward measuring knowledge that middle-class white Americans value and promote. But both parents and teachers should appreciate the arbitrary content of the test. It is not unreasonable to predict that if the printed word becomes subordinate to tape recorders and television as a way of presenting information and knowledge, one hundred years from now our culture might place higher value on "the ability to imagine a visual scene from an input of sounds" than on richness of vocabulary. There may well be a different test of intelligence a century from now because the skills necessary to adapt successfully will have changed, and the groups labeled intelligent in the future may be different from those who have that label today. It will always be the case that some people are better able to adapt to the society in which they live than others, and man is likely to attribute their more successful adaptation to the possession of a set of superior talents. The society will then make a test to measure those talents and label the score as an index of "intelligence." This process will persist as long as man continues to evaluate himself and others. What will change is the list of talents he selects to celebrate.

Is Intelligence Inherited? Since most people believe that intelligence—no matter what its definition—must be related to the organization of the brain, they naturally assume that intellectual ability is inherited and attribute differences in intelligence to hereditary factors. There are several serious conceptual problems attached to this popular belief. First, no psychological characteristic is inherited independent of the specific environment in which a person grows. We know, for example, that if the prenatal environment is altered, hereditary capacities can be changed. Thus, although we all possess the hereditary capacity for two hands, many pregnant women who took thalidomide gave birth to children without hands. Similarly, we can affect the normal influence of heredity by changing the environment after birth. Some children are born with a hereditary capacity to develop diseases like PKU or pellagra, which can lead to serious forms of mental retardation. But by giving the young child a correct diet early in life, the development of such diseases can be prevented. If the effect of heredity can be deflected from its natural direction for the presence of limbs and for mental diseases, it is likely to be alterable for most psychological attributes, including the ability to solve problems on intelligence tests.

The claim that intelligence is inherited finds strength in one indisputable fact. The more similar two people are in their genetic makeup, the more similar their IQ scores. Identical twins, who have the same heredity, are more similar in IQ than fraternal twins or pairs of brothers or sisters. Children are more similar in IQ to their own parents than to the parents of the children next door. However, the fact that similar genetic constitution is accompanied by similarity in IQ does not necessarily imply that IQ must be inherited. Children are also more similar in motives and attitudes to their parents than to unrelated people yet we do not believe that motives and attitudes are inherited. More important, average IQ scores have increased over ten points during the past twenty years, yet it is difficult to believe that the genes that are presumed to determine intelligence have changed over such a short period. Ten percent of all children between the ages of five and eleven increase their IQ scores by as much as fifteen points, and this change seems to be due to motivation, not genes. Since IQ scores are partly a function of motivation and acquired knowledge, final, incontrovertible proof of the influence of heredity on IQ (though not on brain structure) is still lacking.

Finally, it is important to realize that the genetic constitution of a population does not produce a specific level of intellectual ability. Heredity sets a range of ability, and it is primarily relevant to setting the ceiling. It is possible that genetic factors influence exceptional competence at playing the piano, but any normal child can tap out a tune. Genetic factors are likely to be influential in producing a high degree of competence at skills that are unusually difficult to attain, such as exceptional talent at mathematics or music, but they are less critical for attainment of skills that are easy or only moderately difficult.

We believe that reading, writing, and adding are moderately

easy skills, well within the capacity of all children who do not have serious brain damage. Hence genetic differences among racial or ethnic groups may not be of crucial importance with respect to satisfactory performance at school-related tasks. However, Arthur Jensen has made the controversial suggestion that the lower IQ scores of black children as compared with white children may be genetic in origin and call for different curricula and school experiences. This proposition is logically faulty and based on insufficient evidence. The first problem with Jensen's argument is his failure to take into account environmental variables. Since most black children grow up in different environments from white children, it is possible—indeed, likely—that the differences in IQ are attributable to different living conditions rather than to heredity. In order to conclude that genetics were determinate we would have to be sure that the environments of the two groups were identical. A second weakness in Jensen's argument is his assumption that differences in IQ imply a need for different curricula. As we have seen, the tasks taught by the school are not extremely difficult and seem to be within the natural capacities of all human beings regardless of their genetic composition.

What shall we conclude about the meaning of the word "intelligence"? We must acknowledge, first, that at this time in history there are different, legitimate views of the concept, most of which emphasize quality of reasoning and richness of symbols, concepts, and rules. But we are left with the problem of judging "quality" of reasoning. Quality, like beauty, is a relative matter; it depends on the problems posed by a particular cultural setting and the concepts and rules the culture values. We are forced therefore to return to the original theme of intelligence as adaptation to a particular setting. Let us assume that a man's successful adaptation to his society is a function of three kinds of attributes—physical characteristics, cultural values, and mental abilities. A healthy person has the best set of physical and physiological characteristics for the setting in which he lives; a successful person has the right set of values for his culture; an intelligent person possesses the most appropriate set of mental structures and processes—especially, certain concepts and rules—for the problems encountered in his society. From this point of view, the intelligence test is valid, provided that its content is related to the society in which the child lives.

IMPLICATIONS FOR THE TEACHER

It is an unfortunate fact that psychologists and teachers must rely on what they observe in a child's behavior and responses to questions in order to evaluate him. As has been argued throughout this section, the child's behavior in the classroom and his answers to tests or to questions addressed to him are not faithful indexes of the quality of his thought. Thus the teacher should regard the child's written or oral response not as an end in itself but as the first clue to making wise guesses about how much he understands.

Every test score should be viewed with extreme caution, for a wrong answer does not mean that the child does not understand the problem or is incapable of arriving at the correct solution. For example, a young child may say "He goned to the store" instead of "He has gone to the store," but this does not mean that he could not tell us that "goned" is incorrect and "has gone" is correct. Similarly, if a young child is asked to draw a man as well as he can, he often draws the arms attached to the place where the ears should be. However, if he is asked to compare a drawing of a well-formed man with his own drawing and to point to the better of the two, he quickly selects the well-formed representation. *Every child always knows much more than he can produce.*

A child's behavior in a problem situation is controlled by many factors. A careless attitude toward drawing or an inability to coordinate lines can yield a poor reproduction; a poor vocabulary can destroy the effective communication of a well-formed idea. A child's actions and speech are the complex result of many factors, including motivation, language proficiency, expectancy of success, anxiety, and preferred strategies for perceptual analysis or evaluation. The child's final performance on a test is an inadequate index of any one of these processes, for it is a unique composite of them all. *The child has many ways to give a wrong answer.* Perhaps one day we will have more direct access to the child's thoughts and not have to guess their form from his hesitant speech or the cryptic message he writes on paper.

The child's psychological growth is the product of an active attempt to make sense of his experience. The child is not a passive being whose desires, ideas, and skills are molded by the environment.

He continually tries to control uncertainty and prepare for the future. More specifically, he continually tests his knowledge of right and wrong, his skills, his acceptance by others, and his power, attractiveness, and sex-role identity. He thinks naturally and does not need to be continually prodded to solve problems. But in order to think, he needs equipment. The equipment takes the form of the mental structures—schemata, images, symbols, concepts, and rules—that are the basic units of thought. The cognitive processes of perception, memory, generation of ideas, evaluation, and deduction act on these units and form higher-order mental structures that help the child solve more difficult problems. If a problem is central to the child's concern, the processes will be activated naturally. If it is not, the child may not work very hard at solving the problem because he does not have a good reason to do so. The discussion of motivational forces in the first part of this book detailed some of the conditions that help the child to rationalize his involvement in problems he does not care about initially. Since the child is psychologically active, not passive, to the forces imposed on him, it is unlikely that any one curriculum or teaching device will solve, once and for all, the problem of pupil apathy.

Although there are many salutary changes needed in the classroom, it is inaccurate to place the entire burden of responsibility for a child's failure to learn on the public school. To make the school the only culpable agent is scapegoating. First, the child's motivation and attitudes are the most important determinants of his progress. The home, not the school, has the primary influence on these factors. Second, society exerts control over what the school teaches the child. The critics of the school monotonously note that the child on the playground is learning something every day and smiling as he does it. Since this joy is absent in the classroom, the school must be doing something wrong. This conclusion glosses over the important difference between playground and school. The child *decides* what he wants to learn on the playground; he does not decide what he wants to learn in school. Indeed, if multiplication were a skill that children naturally yearned to acquire, we might not have invented the school. The child does not find all tasks equally inviting. The suggestion that all skills are potentially fun for all children contains an important fallacy. The typical child's attitude toward school tasks—in a variety of settings—is negative. There are good reasons for this coolness. As indicated in the first part of this book, the child needs to believe that he is capable of determining his actions and values. This need can be seen in pure form in the four-year-old who fumbles with his shoe-laces and pushes his mother's intruding fingers aside. He wants to do the job himself. If we grant the enormous power of this motive, it follows that the child may initially resist any adult-defined goal, regardless of its content or mode of presentation. If society had no special preferences as to the talents it wanted children to attain, children would obviously be more enthusiastic each morning. They would select tasks in accordance with the values of their peer group, the immediacy of feedback, the likelihood of success, and the degree to which sensory and motor delights were part of the learning experience. Spelling, arithmetic, history, and science would not rank high on their list of preferences. These academic skills were given priority by society, and the decision was partly rational. If we believe in this decision we must tolerate the dissonance generated by the possibility that the child will not agree; we must become less pollyannaish about academic mastery. Speaking, running, and climbing are natural activities that the child wants to perfect; reading, writing, and arithmetic are not.

Hence there is more than a bit of romanticism in some of the harsh and almost totally destructive criticisms of the school. These attacks place the total responsibility for educational failures on the authoritarian and rigid structures and practices of the elementary school system and suggest—dangerously, we believe—that if the child were left completely free he would seek the proper intellectual diet. This conclusion is probably untrue. This writer has observed many unstructured classrooms and has been unimpressed with the motivation for mastery or the intellectual progress of the children in such educational contexts. In one school that stands out clearly, almost half a fourth-grade class of middle-class children was seriously behind normal grade level in reading competence. This would not be a tragedy if the students had developed an exciting proficiency in poetry or gymnastics. But they had not. The classroom was merely a permissive atmosphere in which the child, from first-grade entrance, had not been persuaded to master the subject-matter competences that schools require. The result was a quiet, almost apathetic classroom, not a creative and engaging one.

These remarks should not be misinterpreted as a nineteenth-century plea for tough tactics in the classroom. They are simply a gentle reminder that the young want guidance. Most ten-year-olds reply to the question "Why does the child need parents and teachers when he is young?" with "They tell you the right things to do." The child is as frail as the adult when it comes to selecting an ideology to live by. If a nineteen-year-old college student has difficulty rationalizing intellectual involvement in his courses, it is unlikely that the eight-year-old will be able to do so. He needs as much help as the college sophomore. The plea here is for a firm but gentle shove in the direction of mastery by a teacher who conveys to the child her own love of learning. There is no more attractive incentive than an adult who seems to enjoy what he is doing. The child who wants to feel the same elation will make the reasonable assumption that the use of mind generates the enjoyment, and he will begin to pursue this goal.

A second plea is for surprise. Most children are happy on the first day of school and bored by November first because, as we have known for thousands of years, man enjoys novelty. Unfortunately, both child and adult rapidly adapt to the new and boredom replaces zeal. We must not minimize the serious deficiencies in current educational practices, but we must also appreciate the complexity of the problem. The school is in need of improvement; the child is not completely a blossom; learning to divide is not a joy.

The child, like the adult, thrives on variety he can handle, resents manipulation, desires autonomy, tries to discern his place in the world, and enjoys understanding. Human beings are elated when they use their talents to solve a difficult problem, see a new relation, resolve an inconsistency, or conquer an obstacle. The mission of education is to persuade each child that he is a richer source of ideas than he suspects and to enable him to experience the exhilaration that is inherent in the creative use of mind.

Bennett, E. M., and Cohen, L. R. Men and women: personality patterns and contrast. *Genet. Psychol. Monogr.*, 1959, 60, 101–53.

Craig, R. C. Observation versus participation in learning to discover. Presented at a meeting of the AERA (American Educational Research Association), Chicago, February, 1968.

Daniel, K. B. The effects of immediate and delayed reinforcement with respect to knowledge of test results. Presented at a meeting of the AERA, Chicago, February, 1968.

Gibson, E. Development of perception: discrimination of depth compared with discrimination of graphic symbols. In J. C. Wright and J. Kagan (eds.), *Basic Cognitive Processes in Children,* Monograph of the Society for Research in Child Development, 1963, 28: 2, 5–32.

Goethals, G. W., and Klos, D. *Experiencing Youth,* Boston, Little, Brown, 1970.

Gotkin, L. G. A calendar curriculum for disadvantaged kindergarten children. *Teaching College Record,* 1967, 68, 406–16.

Hardy, G. E. *Citation for Children,* New York, 1892.

Iwai, H., and Reynolds, D. K. Morita psychotherapy: views from the West. *Am. J. Psychiat.,* 1970, 126:7, 1031–36.

John, E. R., Chessler, P., Bartlett, F., and Victor, I. Observation learning in cats. *Science,* 1968, 159, 1489–91.

Kagan, J. The child's sex role classification of school objects. *Child Devel.,* 1964, 35, 1051–56.

Kagan, J., Hosken, B., and Watson, S. The child's symbolic conceptualization of the parents. *Child Devel.,* 1961, 32, 625–36.

Kagan, J., and Moss, H. A. *Birth to Maturity,* New York, Wiley, 1962.

Lansdell, H. The use of factor scores from the Wechsler-Bellevue Scale of Intelligence in assessing patients with temporal lobe removals. *Cortex,* 1968, 4, 257–68.

Maccoby, E. E. Selective auditory attention in children. In L. P. Lipsitt and C. C. Spiker (eds.), *Advances in Child Development and Behavior,* New York, Academic Press, 1967.

Messer, S. B. The effect of anxiety over intellectual performance on reflective and impulsive children. Unpublished
doctoral dissertation, Harvard University, 1968.

Osgood, C. E. The cross-cultural generality of visual-verbal
synesthetic tendencies. *Behav. Sci.*, 1960, 5, 146–69.

Piaget, J. *The Origins of Intelligence in Children*, New York,
International Universities Press, 1952.

Piaget, J. *Play, Dreams, and Imitation*, New York, Norton,
1951.

Prince, R. The therapeutic process in cross-cultural perspective.
Am. J. Psychiat., 1968, 124:9, 1171–83.

Ratoosh, P. Experimental studies of implementation. In J. R.
Lawrence (ed.), *Operational Research and the Social
Sciences*, London, Tavistock, 1966.

Ryan, F. L. The effectiveness of teacher involvement in a programmed social studies sequence. Presented at a meeting
of the AERA, Chicago, February, 1968.

Sassenrath, J. M., and Yonge, G. D. Effects of delayed information feedback and feedback cues in learning on delayed
retention. *J. Ed. Psychol.*, 1969, 60, 174–77.

Seligman, M. E. P., and Maier, S. F. Failure to escape traumatic shock. *J. Exper. Psychol.*, 1967, 74, 1–9.

Stretch, R., Orloff, E. R., and Dalrymple, S. D. Maintenance
of responding by fixed-interval schedules of electric shock,
presented in squirrel monkeys. *Science*, 1968, 162, 583–85.

Valins, S., and Ray, A. A. Effects of cognitive desensitization on
avoidance behavior. *J. Person. and Soc. Psychol.*, 1967, 7,
345–50.

Wallach, M. A., and Kogan, N. *Modes of Thinking in Young
Children*, New York, Holt, Rinehart & Winston, 1965.

White, S. H. Changes in learning processes in the late preschool years. Presented at a meeting of the AERA, Chicago, February, 1968.

Wodtke, K. H., Brown, B. R., Sands, H. R., and Fredericks, P.
The effects of subject matter and individual difference variables on learning from scrambled versus ordered instruc-
tional programs. Presented at a meeting of the AERA, Chicago, February, 1968.

Yondo, R. M., and Kagan, J. The effect of teacher tempo on
the child. *Child Devel.*, 1968, 39, 27–34.

Index

B   1
C   2
D   3
E   4
F   5
G   6
H   7
I   8
J   9